The **LIFE** Pocket Guide to

DIGITAL
PHOTOGRAPHY

D0968009

LIFE Books
Managing Editor **Robert Sullivan**
Editorial Operations Manager
Brian Fellows
Copy Editors
Kathleen Berger, Parlan McGaw

Book packaged by **Moseley Road Inc.**
President Sean Moore
Art Director Brian MacMullen
Editorial Director Lisa Purcell
Editor Amber Rose

Revised edition produced by
Kensington Media Group, Inc.
President Morin Bishop
Art Director Barbara Chilenskas

Joe McNally Studio
Lynn DelMastro
Drew Gurian
Lynda Peckham
Will Foster
Karen Lenz
Mike Grippi
Mike Cali

Published by LIFE Books, an imprint
of Time Home Entertainment Inc.
135 West 50th Street
New York, New York 10020

ISBN 13: 978-1-60320-935-9
ISBN 10: 1-60320-935-2

If you would like to order any of our hardcover
Collector's Edition books, please call us at
1-800-327-6388. (Monday through Friday,
7:00 a.m.— 8:00 p.m. or Saturday,
7:00 a.m.— 6:00 p.m. Central Time).

Time Home Entertainment
Publisher **Jim Childs**

Vice President, Business Development
& Strategy **Steven Sandonato**
Executive Director, Marketing Services
Carol Pittard
Executive Director, Retail & Special Sales
Tom Mifsud
Executive Publishing Director **Joy Butts**
Director, Bookazine Development
& Marketing **Laura Adam**
Finance Director **Glenn Buonocore**
Associate Publishing Director **Megan Pearlman**
Assistant General Counsel **Helen Wan**
Assistant Director, Special Sales
Ilene Schreider
Book Production Manager **Suzanne Janso**
Design & Prepress Manager
Anne-Michelle Gallero
Brand Manager **Roshni Patel**
Associate Production Manager
Kimberly Marshall
Associate Prepress Manager
Alex Voznesenskiy
Assistant Brand Manager
Stephanie Braga

Editorial Director **Stephen Koepp**
Editorial Operations Director
Michael Q. Bullerdick

Photography copyright © Joe McNally except as noted
(Back cover photo, page 6, and pages
128–129 by Drew Gurian; page 20 by Milos Luzanin/
Shutterstock.com; page 34 by Doug Karcher; page 136
by Andrew Tomasino)

Cover Design by Barbara Chilenskas

We welcome your comments and suggestions about
LIFE Books.
Please write to us at:
LIFE Books
Attention: Book Editors
PO Box 11016
Des Moines, IA 50336-1016

Special thanks to: Christine Austin, Katherine Barnet,
Jeremy Biloon, Susan Chodakiewicz, Rose Cirrincione,
Lauren Hall Clark, Jacqueline Fitzgerald, Christine Font,
Jenna Goldberg, Hillary Hirsch, David Kahn,
Amy Mangus, Robert Marasco, Amy Migliaccio, Nina
Mistry, Dave Rozzelle, Adriana Tierno, Vanessa Wu

The 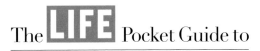 Pocket Guide to

DIGITAL PHOTOGRAPHY

Everything you need to shoot like the pros

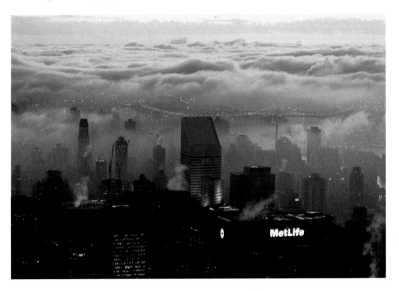

by Joe McNally

Winner of the Alfred Eisenstaedt Award for Magazine Photography

Foreword by John Loengard

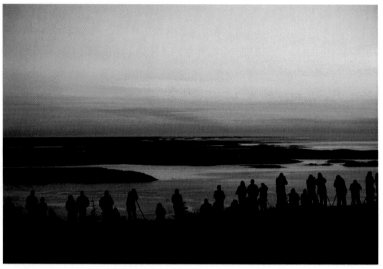

Photographers at sunrise, Maine, 70MM, 1/13TH AT F/5.6, ISO 200

DEDICATION
This book is for those who went before. To what they saw, and how
they saw it. And to the fact that, sometimes at great peril, in impossible
conditions, with all odds against them, they shot it well and beautifully,
and shared it with us. Their work is the stuff of all our memories.
—Joe McNally

CONTENTS

Foreword: The Right Photographer, the Right Guide **6**
Introduction: Welcome to Our Book **8**

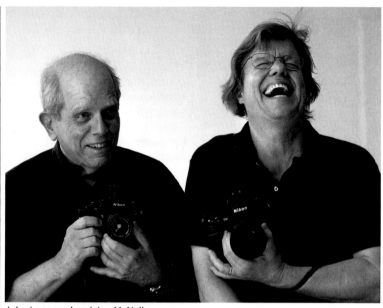

John Loengard and Joe McNally

FOREWORD
The right photographer, the right guide

Nearly 75 years ago, four photographers were listed on the masthead of the first issue of LIFE magazine. They, and the technical wizards who followed them on the staff, were quite willing to explain how they took their eye-catching pictures. They felt there was little danger of being copied. "A good photograph is one that can't be repeated," says Harry Benson. What mattered was catching the moment, and each LIFE photographer felt he or she knew how to do that better than anyone else. Joe McNally, the 90th (and last) photographer to join LIFE's staff, brings this benign egoism into the digital age.

McNally is a talented photographer with a wise voice. He once draped movie star Michelle Pfeiffer with diamonds and, on a separate occasion, he talked the U.S. Olympic water polo team into posing naked for a LIFE cover. He writes in a friendly, conversational tone that makes him an ideal choice to pen a guide for the beginning photographer. His pictures speak for themselves.

This is a beautiful book, but McNally's advice is not limited to amateurs. He has never been to the moon. If he were to go, he would point out that, on the near side, we see that the light is the same as on the beach at Malibu or in the Hamptons. Working on the moon's far, dark side is a problem. I'd really like to know what advice he'd offer. He knows from experience what is important in photography and what's just distraction.

With today's digital cameras, photography appears to be as complicated as boiling an egg (which is not quite so simple as you might think, of course—a two-minute egg in Denver being quite different from a two-minute egg in New York City). Indeed, as McNally explains, digital cameras can be used to skirt such problems as focus, color balance and exposure that long bedeviled even the greatest photographers of the past. And we do not have to wait for days to see if the picture came out. There are even little gyroscopes built into lenses to counteract the shakiness of our hands. Those of us who worked with film in the 20th century can only smack our foreheads and exclaim how easy things would have been if we'd had digital way back when. We are free today to concentrate on timing and perspective, on quality of light and composition. All of these topics McNally discusses at the proper length.

Still, I should add a note of caution. "You could have the most modern cameras and not see picture possibilities," the wonderful LIFE photographer Alfred Eisenstaedt told me when he was 94 years old. "I see picture possibilities in many things. I could stay for hours and watch a raindrop. I see pictures all the time. I think like this."

So does Joe McNally. And you should, too.

—John Loengard
Acclaimed photographer John Loengard joined LIFE's staff in 1961 and later became the magazine's seventh picture editor, as well as the founding picture editor of People *magazine.*

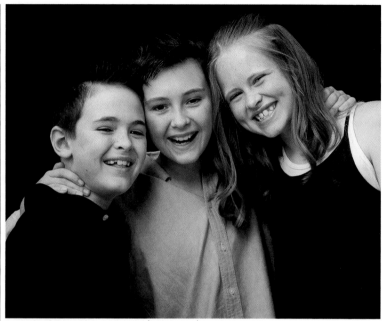

Portrait of three kids, 150mm, 1/250th at f/8, ISO 200

INTRODUCTION
Welcome to our book

THE DEMOCRACY OF DIGITAL

*I've been doing this for a long time—I've been living in this world
we call* photography *for a long, long time—and I remember a few
things from the old days. The olden days. The days of yore.*

*Photography used to be not for the faint of heart. Its rigors
would weed out the not-so-committed pretty quickly. You had to
crank the f-stop ring yourself! And you often had to focus*

lenses that were so slow and dark, it was like peering down a side alley through a dirty window. Then you needed a basement or a bathtub, plumbing, tubes, clamps, drainage, pans, reels, chemicals, red lights, clothespins, special paper and drying racks—just to see what you thought you just shot. Many times, you were wrong about what you thought you'd just shot.

You also needed a good-sized chunk of that amazing thing we always seemed to run out of: time.

There was a tremendous gulf between the pro and the enthusiast. Ansel Adams rattled around the Southwest with his battered truck and his view camera, which looked like a giant accordion with a lens attached to it. Richard Avedon shot legendary beauties in Manhattan lofts and was therefore worshipped by fashionistas and attended to by legions of assistants. There were these luminaries, these magicians, and then there was pretty much everybody else, punting along with Brownies or Instamatics, making hopeful trips to the drugstore and generally picking up packages filled with disappointment a week or so later.

It all seemed pretty hard, right? And unfair.

Now we live in a place and age I refer to as the Democracy of Digital. Technology has eliminated the basement darkroom and the whole notion of photography as an intense labor of love for obsessives and replaced them with a sense of immediacy and instant gratification. Shoot the picture; look at the picture. Shoot and look, shoot and look. If it doesn't look good, shoot again. And again . . . and again. It's just reusable ones and zeroes now, not frames of film winding around in a cassette, each cassette with a processing price tag.

The result has been like turning a two-lane country road traveled by just a hardy few into a multilane superhighway, with lots and lots of folks driving fancy machines real, real fast—even if they don't have a clue where they're going.

Digital technology has thrown a closed shop wide open, and there are more people out there snapping away than ever before. Some of the pictures are bad, some of them are good and many of them need some seasoning and direction. But the point is, a lot of people are doing photography— there are record numbers of shooters everywhere.

Presumably, if you have this book in your hands, you're one of them. Perhaps you've been at it a while but feel you could take better pictures. Maybe you just got the camera. You found it under the tree or you received it for your birthday or you bought it yourself after much agonizing about which of the myriad models out there might suit your fancy, your visual ambition and your budget.

You found during your research that digital photography is a fast-moving river; you just have to jump in at some point and start swimming. No more waiting to see if a new, snazzier model is coming out next month. You already know it is, and it will have 20 or 30 million more pixels than the model you bought today. No matter. You now have a camera, which is this miracle device you've been longing for, a tool designed to catch, record and interpret light. To freeze a moment and a memory. And this magical instrument can go with you everywhere.

In our blog-mad, tweeting, Facebooking, Citizen Journalist world, where everybody out there is screaming in one way or another NOTICE *ME!*, this digital camera is not just required of the ardent hobbyist, it is needed by just about everyone. You record, therefore you are. In one way or another—be it in a blog or on Flickr or in an electronic album that you put together for the family and then print— you publish. You share your news with the world. The airwaves no longer belong to networks. The news is no longer gathered and disseminated by the select few. You are the news. You are the editor and publisher of your own life and times. And just like any cranky, old-time newspaper editor with a hole to fill in the Metro section, you need pictures to go with the story.

So, let's make them good pictures, shall we?

GETTING STARTED

As I said at the top, I've been doing this a long time, but I haven't yet lost so many memory cells that I don't remember way back when. I can still recall those first, awkward, fumbling attempts with a camera that was, in its basic way, far simpler to operate than today's digital marvels—if you choose to employ all the latest bells and whistles. Back then, I would shoot, then curse, knowing I had just missed a moment. Then I would curse some more back in the

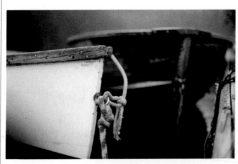

Two boats, 50MM, 1/2500TH AT F/1.4, ISO 200

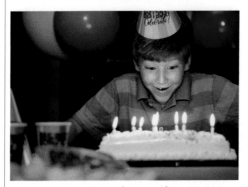

Birthday party, 125mm, 1/60th at f/2.8, ISO 800

darkroom when what drifted up to me through the liquid in the tray looked nothing like what my overreaching mind and imagination had hoped for when I'd clicked.

You know something? I still get frustrated. I still shout at the rain and the sun and the wind when they conspire against my aspirations. When I'm frustrated, I entirely forget the time just last week when the sun and wind and a light rain all worked in concert for me, as if I were a conductor with a baton standing before the natural elements, not a plain ol' photog with a camera.

The simple truth of it is that even the most experienced shooters still miss the moment, still make mistakes—sometimes mistakes so basic that they wonder if there's ever any way to really and reliably learn this art and craft.

In this way, digital photography is no different from old-time photography. Good pictures are good pictures; you make some, you miss some. Not all of the photographs on the following pages were shot digitally, but those that weren't were selected because they could have been. Digital has changed the game, to be sure, but as in sports, the same rule applies eternally: The one who performs best—the one with the most points—wins. Whether we're talking football or tennis or photography, you play the game the right way, you win. I hope some of the info and tips that follow allow you to win more than you lose.

It's an unfortunate truth that the magic box you just feverishly unpacked is a machine designed to do two things—make pictures and drive you mad. But here's the thing: If you didn't care, you wouldn't get upset, right? If you weren't passionate and determined about all of this, you would just put your camera down like yesterday's newspaper. But you can't, just like I can't, all these years downstream.

Remember this: Good pictures demand care, and truly good pictures are hard to make. The manufacturers are out there selling us the digital dream, telling us that the camera does it all. And some of these machines almost do; they are marvelous contraptions. But no matter how fancy the gear, photography itself, at the end of the day, rules. Just like Mother Nature, the photo gods are mercurial indeed and smile upon us only occasionally and reluctantly.

So relax. You will make mistakes! As someone much smarter than I once said, "Failure is a form of progress." He must have been thinking about photography.

DO THESE THINGS FIRST:

❐ Take the camera out of the box and attach the shoulder strap. I generally put a little bit of gaffer tape (not duct tape, but photographer's gaffer tape) around the tails of the strap so they don't flap around and slip.

❐ Fully charge the battery. It usually comes from the manufacturer only partially loaded.

❐ Don't read the manual right away. You'll either get discouraged or fall asleep.

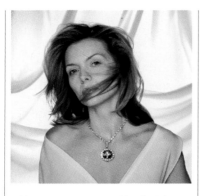

Michelle Pfeiffer wearing the Hope Diamond, 150MM, 1/250TH AT F/8, ISO 100

- ❐ Most cameras come with a "quick guide" designed to get you taking pictures right away. Do read that.

- ❐ Make sure you have either the cord to connect the camera directly to your computer or some sort of card reader by which you can pull your images off the card and onto your desktop.

- ❐ Make sure you have some sort of browsing software so you can take a look at the pictures. Many digital cameras come with viewing software bundled with the hardware. If yours doesn't, there are many, many fairly simple, not-too-expensive viewing programs out there.

- ❐ Then, put the camera on P. It stands for "program," but it is also jokingly referred to as "perfect" or "professional." No matter. In this mode, you let the camera drive, and for your first few spins, that's a good strategy. Most of these cameras have such a high level of technology and sophistication that they will sort things out for you very well, without you expending any thought (or sweat) whatsoever.

THIS ALLOWS YOU TO...

Have fun! Picture-making can be hard to do, yes, but it shouldn't be in any way miserable. Shoot pictures. Look at the hits, near misses and complete disasters. Make some more of them. Get used to the feel of the camera.

Many cameras now come with a "kit" lens, a reasonably decent, all-purpose zoom that goes pretty wide to sorta telephoto. Work both ends of the lens, and see what the wide view and telephoto view can do for you. Start thinking about when it might be suitable to use one or the other.

Put yourself in different situations: bright sun, interiors, birthday parties, on the sidelines of ball games. See how the camera handles all this nutty stuff you see out there, the stuff that constitutes your world. Continue to shoot; take lots of pictures. Remember, you don't have to run to the drugstore to develop these. No pixels have to die! If something is intriguing enough to make you lift your camera to your eye, then it is worth making 50 pictures of it, not just 5. Shoot! You will only get better at this after you do it repeatedly. Many folks have asked me over the years how I got to be a LIFE photographer—how I got to be a guy who actually gets Michelle Pfeiffer to pose for his camera. The question always reminds me of that old joke about the lost tourist in Manhattan asking a New Yorker, "How do I get to Carnegie Hall?"

Reply? "Practice!"

After shooting many, many pictures on P, you upload them to your computer and find yourself with a bunch of thumbnails in front of you on your screen. Look at them. Which ones move your head and your heart? Which are utterly without redeeming content? Which are in between?

Now, after this process, your compass has been set. To a degree. Now's the time to read the manual. Or read this book. It's a lot less boring than the manual.

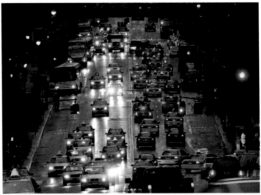

City street at dusk, 600MM, 1/30TH AT F/11, ISO 800

A FEW THINGS TO KNOW RIGHT OFF THE BAT

There won't be a test at the end of this book, but there are some photography basics and terms that you should know as you navigate your way through it. Yes, there's a glossary in the back—of course there is—and some of these intro concepts will be covered back there, too. But these items are good to get under your belt now. I've listed below the barest few concepts and technical terms. Come on back here if you need a little memory refresher as you travel through the pages that follow.

First we have the word **aperture**. This is an adjustable, circular opening inside the lens that regulates how much light goes through the lens and hits the sensor. It's basically a hole in the lens that you can control by making it bigger or smaller. Small hole, very little light gets to the sensor. Big hole, and the lens becomes like an open water main with light pouring through it. This is your light spigot.

And now let's explain **exposure**. This is the end of, and extension of, the aperture equation. This is how much light hits the sensor, and for how long (two things you have control over). You'll hear the terms "bad exposure" and "good exposure" all the time. You'll hear "underexposed" and "overexposed" as long as you shoot. With practice, you will produce more good than bad, fewer overs and unders.

Generally, the exposure is described by the time it took to make the picture, plus the amount of light you were allowing in. For example, you'd say, "I shot that at 1/60th at f/5.6 and ISO 400."

What?!

Okay: The 1/60th is 1/60th of a

second. This is the **shutter speed**—easily understood as the duration of the exposure. Fast speeds are usually 1/250th of a second on up to 1/8000th of a second, and these fast shutter speeds are generally used in bright conditions. Darker environments demand slower shutter speeds, ranging down from 1/30th of a second or so all the way to 8 or 10 seconds, depending on subject matter. Shutter speed is a critical issue because it will directly affect how sharp your photos are. The slower the shutter, the greater the chance of camera shake. Shooting sharp at slow shutter speeds requires practice, a steady hand and, sometimes, a tripod.

The f/5.6 in the notation above brings us to **f-stops** (or **f-numbers**). These define how wide your aperture is open or closed. They are the clicks on your camera's aperture dial. Among the most common are f/2.8, f/4, f/5.6, f/8, f/11 and f/16. These are "full" stops of light. Each f-stop number is 1.4 f times larger than the one preceding it, and each full click from one stop to the next either doubles the light going through the lens or cuts it in half, depending on which way you are clicking. The smaller numbers, somewhat counterintuitively, denote the larger lens openings. Conversely, the larger the f-number, the smaller the lens opening. Go figure. Here's a handy alliteration I once heard to remember this formula: Large (numbers), less light. LLL!

Now what was that last thing: **ISO**? This refers to the sensitivity of the chip, or sensor, and expresses in numeric fashion the "speed" at which the sensor will accept light. High ISO numbers, such as 1600, will enable photography in low-light conditions. In bright sun, ISO 100 or 200 is plenty. "ISO" comes from the International Organization for Standardization. This organization defines how these standards are determined.

The last term I would like to touch on here before we march forth is **white balance**. Light has color, and different lights have different colors. Daylight has different color casts, depending on time of day and atmospheric conditions. Fluorescent and tungsten, or incandescent, bulbs give off shades of green and yellow, respectively. Digital cameras can compensate for these different colors, and you can adjust for them on the fly with a flick of a button.

There's a world of weird color out there; you have to sort it out at the lens, and program your camera accordingly.

THE BEST WAY TO USE THIS BOOK

Well, it's not *War and Peace*. And I hope it's not *Crime and Punishment*. So you don't have to read it front to back, although you certainly could.

It's a guide, which is to say it's got a lot of how-tos, a bunch of pictures to illustrate my points and a ton of tips. It has a glossary, as we've mentioned, and an index, and you can and should refer to them regularly when your memory of a particular term falters, or when you want to zoom in on "zoom lenses." I have tried to structure the book so that it eases you into

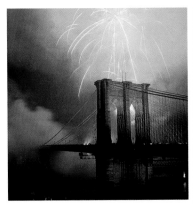

Part One: Light

photography: Here's how to expose a picture correctly; here's how to work your lenses; and now, here's how to get a little fancy. But life in the world of photography does not always proceed in a linear fashion, and so you might want some guidance on composition, which is way back in Part Five, even before you want to start goofing around with exotic lenses. Perfectly okay, and please do skip around. As you'll see in the pages that follow, I'm not big on rules.

Still, it's prudent to build a foundation when approaching anything new. Here's a not-so-sneak preview of what's coming up.

We deal first with light—what's good light, what's bad light and is there a way to turn bad light into good light. (There sure is!) The stars of **Part One**, as pertains to your camera, are what I call the holy trinity of an exposure: **aperture** (how wide or

how closed or small), **shutter speed** (how fast or slow it should be) and **ISO**. We will learn, in this part of the book, how to balance this triumvirate of adjustable factors to allow just the right amount of light in for just the right period of time. There are many things that you could describe as the be-all and end-all of photography, including composition or color (or lack thereof). But for most of us, the be-all and end-all is light and the ability to use it to make a good, sharp exposure. And so we begin here.

In **Part Two** we look at—and through—the eye of the camera, **the lens**. This is the instrument that drinks in not only light but the subject matter as well, and sends this information on to the camera's sensor. First off, we'll discuss depth of field—what's in focus where (in the background or foreground or both) and why you might want one effect or another, and how to achieve it. Then we start playing with toys: wide-angles, zooms, telephotos. I think you'll be interested to see how each lens pertains not

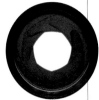

Part Two: The Lens

only to the kind of photography you might guess it pertains to—this kind of lens is for macro shooting, and that one's for when you're far away—but can also produce many different results in a variety of situations. As I said, these are toys. It's fun to play around. In **Part Three**, Design Elements, I'm going to ask you to look hard at what's in the lens. You don't want to just line things up; you don't want to just focus, click and record. You want to produce an interesting, entertaining picture—even if it's just of little Julie blowing out the candles. What are the textures in the image, and how might you choose the right one to emphasize? What patterns do you see, and could this triangular shape in the left half direct the viewer to the precise spot you want him or her to focus on? Don't worry, this isn't geometry class. Design elements are more fun than that.

Part Four is one I'm partial to: **Color**. I'm a color guy, as you'll learn. I do appreciate and occasionally choose black-and-white because it inarguably possesses unique qualities that convey, in photography, certain moods and emotions. We'll surely discuss all that, and I hope that I can hint at when black-and-white may be, sometimes surprisingly, the way to go. But I'm no B&W aesthete. I like gaudy color and subtle color, muted color and mad color. The capturing and employment of color is, of course, an adjunct to how we deal with light. By Part Four, we'll know how to handle that. So let's get colorful.

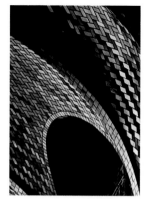

Part Three: Design Elements

And we next arrive at **Part Five**, Composition. If something else hadn't already claimed the be-all and end-all title, this surely would. This is it, isn't it? This is where you play the painter. You know what expressions of light and color are appropriate for this picture, and now comes the big question: What do you include in your canvas?

A quick note here: So far, we've been talking about f-stops and ISOs and all these ways to take good pictures with a digital rig that you can play around with—and that is what our book is going to be mostly about. But we're not going to ignore you point-and-shoot and cell-phone photogs in these pages. Anytime you look in a viewfinder (*any* viewfinder), you can take your best shot or your second-best shot. The choice is yours. When I talk about composition, I'm talking to all of you.

Now, then: Here we discuss the famous **Rule of Thirds**, which allows you, every time you put the camera to your eye, to situate that rectangular view perfectly to draw the viewer's eye whither you will. You divide the field into sections, think things through and then put your subject in an interesting place—often not the center,

Part Four: Color

although sometimes the center—and then and only then, click! Lenses come into play again—this might be cool from a wide angle, this could be cool up close—and we talk about all sorts of portraiture: classic, environmental, group. Your kid's

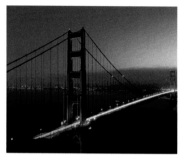

Part Five: Composition

peewee soccer team is a portrait, not just a snap, and you can make it a better one by taking 20 additional seconds to arrange the kids and consider what's in your viewfinder before you press that shutter.

Compose yourself, compose the picture. **Part Six** of the book might easily have been Part One because it's just some last hints and tips that could have been first hints and tips: how to hold the camera, how to walk with a camera, et cetera. You'll find your own way, I'm sure—maybe you already have—but these suggestions are what's worked for me. I think they might help you. If not, forget we ever talked.

One last thing about this particular guide (which is another way of saying "as opposed to the hundred other guides out there"): In each of these sections of the book, you're going to see, first, pages with a white background, and then pages with a bold blue border. It might not be obvious, but the former have the nut and bolts and the how-tos, and the latter have the experiential stuff (plus some more useful how-tos). The editors of LIFE, enablers that they are, have encouraged me to draw on what some would call "my years of experience" and try to get you not only better at photography, but also psyched about it. They've heard my war stories over and over, and they felt it was about time I inflicted them on someone else.

And so I have. That someone else is you.

But I've selectively chosen the stories, and I hope each one inspires you to think about another way, another approach— or, even, an instance when you simply have to play within the rules. That happens, too.

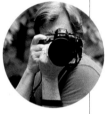

Part Six: Joe's Last Tips

I hope what comes through in all of these stories, or at least in the sum of them, is that I've had fun along the winding way that has been my journey through the world of photography. That's what I wish for you above all else as you unwrap that package and open the box with the gleaming toy inside. Smile first, then withdraw the camera, lift it to your eye, and prepare to . . .

Have fun!

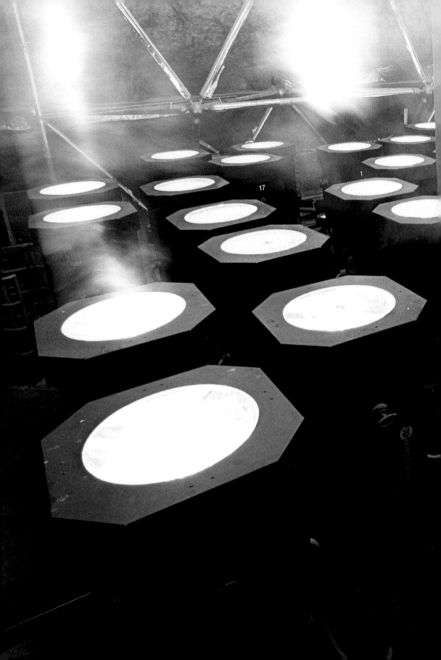

PART ONE
Light

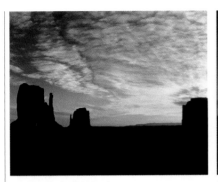

Monument Valley, Utah,
28MM, 1/15TH AT F/11, ISO 100

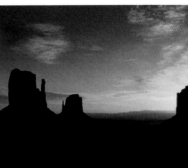

Monument Valley, Utah,
28MM, 1/10TH AT F/11, ISO 100

EXPOSURE

When you take a picture, you can say you just took a "shot," or a "frame," or an "exposure." All of those expressions are true, perhaps none more true than the term exposure. When you go click, what you are doing is exposing photo sensitive material (used to be film, now it's pixels) to light. The light transits the lens of the camera to the sensor via the aperture, which has already been discussed in our introduction as a hole of varying size in the lens. (This hole is also referred to as a diaphragm.)

● How much light hits that sensor is regulated by the size of the aperture and the length of time the sensor is seeing light. That very crucial timing factor is regulated by the camera's shutter, which will stay open for a very brief or quite long period of time. Exactly how long or short that gateway to the sensor is open is called "shutter speed."

We're not quite done. A third factor is always present in the making of an exposure: ISO speed (the initials come from the International Organization for Standardization, as we've learned). The ISO, to reiterate, refers to the camera's sensitivity to light. Predictably, the higher the ISO number, the more sensitive the camera's pixels will be and the less light is needed to take the picture. A lower ISO number means less sensitivity, which translates into the need to operate in brighter conditions.

There you have it: The holy trinity of any exposure—aperture, shutter speed and ISO. These factors have been in play, in concert, ever since 1826, when Nicéphore Niépce poked a camera obscura out of the window

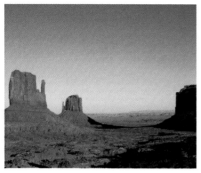

Monument Valley, Utah,
28MM, 1/125TH AT F/11, ISO 100

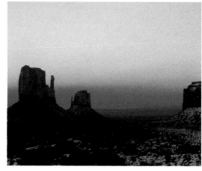

Monument Valley, Utah,
28MM, 1/4TH AT F/11, ISO 100

of his workroom in the French countryside and made an eight-hour exposure, generally recognized as the first photo. Niépce's aperture was a hole in a box, and his pixels a pewter plate covered with bitumen. He let sunlight pour onto it for all that time because he rightly guessed that his "film" had a very low ISO.

Now we have cameras that do all these things for us, automatically. Set the camera on program mode, or P, and let the machine decide. Most of the higher-end digital cameras out there today decide relatively correctly, at least some of the time, what to do. So why bother knowing all this stuff?

Because we humans can do better. Understanding ISO is crucial for any photographer because the camera is a machine without a scintilla of artistic intent or taste. It renders an exposure based on how its mechanical programming reacts to what the lens sees. When confronted with an average scene with even illumination, a camera will most likely perform quite admirably. Stress it a little bit by introducing extremes of either amount or direction of light, and, oh my, that fancy pixel machine can get downright befuddled—and rather quickly.

Put the camera on P mode, for instance, and stand Grandma in front of a brightly lit window and shoot her picture while facing the lens toward the window. The camera reacts to the sunlit window, exposing accordingly. Bye-bye, Grandma!

Likewise, imagine a scene where your daughter, who has a beautiful voice, is singing a solo onstage. A bright spotlight bathes her in a luminous glow, while the rest of the stage dims to utter blackness. With only a limited zoom lens, from your seat in row four, your daughter is a tiny piece of the scene. Most of what the camera sees is the black stage. Again, bye-bye. The camera reacts to all that darkness and opens up the exposure. Your poor kid ends up as burnt pixels, glowing and unrecognizable—even to you.

Look at the four pictures of Monument Valley, Utah, on the preceeding two pages. They are exposed for various effects: to capture the sky and throw the buttes into silhouette, or to show detail of the rock and let the sky lose vibrancy—the holy trinity at play. Same place, same rocks. But different light, different exposure, and—most important—different moods and emotions.

Here's the deal: Think of the camera as a very expensive blender. It takes in everything it sees, dumps it into its computerized brain and spits back to you what it thinks is the right exposure. Call it an educated guess. That's why you have to learn how to control exposure yourself. You don't want to feel like you're spinning a roulette wheel every time you pick up a camera. Read on.

COMPONENTS OF LIGHT

The big three of light are quality, color and direction. These three things are components of any light you may see. Think of all the adjectives used to describe light—bright, harsh, soft, pale, dim. Backlight. Frontlight. Sidelight. Low light. Warm, cool. Not to mention slashing, angled, hard, sumptuous, rich, hot, beautiful, contrasty, smoky, blazing, big, bounced, shaded . . . You could fill a romance novel!

● The real reason we talk of light in such ornate language is the very fact that for us, as photographers, light is language. It's how we, well, tell stories. It's how we flatter our subjects—or not. It has all the flavors of those words above: tone, inflection, color, emotion. You can make someone look like an angel, or look like the devil, depending on the light you use.

THE QUALITY, COLOR AND DIRECTION OF LIGHT

To speak effectively in this language, you need to know how to recognize the big three—and learn how to manipulate them.

First up: the quality of light. Is it soft or hard? Does it create harsh shadows, or does it drape easily on the scene? What kind of light works best for what you are trying to shoot? There are times of the day—for example, high noon on a sunny day—when the light is so unforgiving that it is generally advisable to beat a hasty retreat indoors or under trees or beneath the shadows of buildings. There you can find the beaming sun filtered or tamed and you can work with it, carefully (more on this later). There are other times, say, sunset, when the light is so beautiful you stay out as long as possible, and you literally can't click the shutter fast enough.

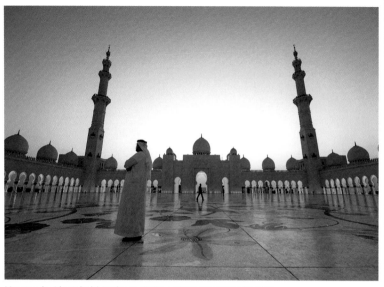

Mosque in Abu Dhabi at dawn, 19MM, 1/25TH AT F/5.6, ISO 200

Light has color. The sunrise and sunset times of day are often referred to as "golden hours," for their warm, richly beautiful glow. As the day progresses, color drains from the light, and the high, hard daylight relentlessly bleaches the richness of color away. If cloud cover comes in, the light filtering through those clouds turns cooler. But the very softness of the cloudy daylight allows the colors out there on the street to return, rendering them rich and saturated.

Light also picks up the color of what it hits. Light bouncing back off a red barn will be distinctly ruddy. Hard daylight pouring in a kitchen window and ricocheting off a natural wood floor will fill the room with a warm, yellow glow.

And what about cityscapes at night? Fuhgeddaboudit! There's fluorescent, tungsten, mercury and sodium vapor—all of them vying for the title of "most obnoxious." These lights end up in the sickly yellow-green part of the spectrum.

Later in this book, we'll get around to programming camera white balance in response to all these teeming color possibilities. For now, just remember that it's essential to watch the light and discern its color.

Finally, light has direction. This is the easy one to spot. Where's the light coming from? Which way do the

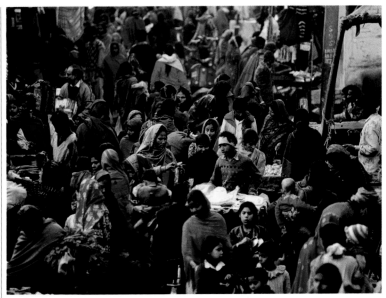

Soft light on a New Delhi street, 200MM, 1/100TH AT F/5.6, ISO 100

shadows fall? Are there shadows at all, or is the quality of light so diffuse and soft that they have disappeared completely? Direction of light teams up with quality and color to hand you, the shooter, either sublime opportunities or a troublesome problem to solve. Let's take a look at some examples.

SOFT LIGHT
Soft, cloudy daylight graces the New Delhi street above with a lovely quality that lets colors speak. Faces remain open, unhidden by the shadows that strong sunlight would produce. This is perfect street-shooting light, if you are looking to do informal portraits or details. Soft light is easy light to work in.

HARD LIGHT
When the sun is high with no cloud cover, the quality of light is crazy hard and the shadows are as sharp as knives. That doesn't mean the light can't be worked. You just have to be selective. This is not light for portraits: Eyes will turn into black shadow pools. But for graphic impact and intensity, raw sun has real appeal and power. Look for shadow play as people move through the streets. Expose for the highlights, and let shadows go black— because they're going there anyway.

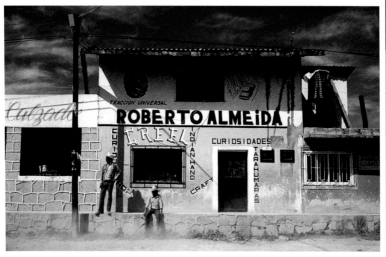

Hard light, Los Mochis, Mexico, 35MM, 1/250TH AT F/11, ISO 64

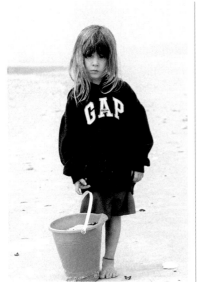

Soft light at the beach,
50MM, 1/125TH AT F/5.6, ISO 100

SOFT LIGHT ON SNOW OR BEACH

I offer this as a notion to tuck away. Soft light is nice light, right? We've already seen that. But, admittedly, it can be a little boring. What will give it that extra edge? What may add just a little more flavor? Sand and snow, those summer and winter delights for anyone who has kids, are the answer. To children, these are things to sled on or make castles out of. To the photog mom or dad, these surfaces can become a "fill card," a huge, natural reflector. This little bit of extra light bounced from below (obviously snow has more bounce than sand) can make for wonderful portrait possibilities.

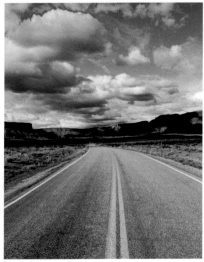

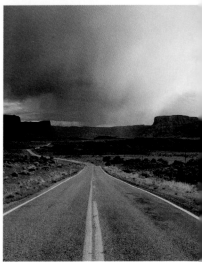

Moab, Utah, 24MM, 1/800TH AT F/10, ISO 200

Moab, Utah, 24MM, 1/50TH AT F/11, ISO 200

[A WALK IN THE EXPOSURE WOODS]

DO THIS FIRST

To make a manual exposure, you need to set the aperture, shutter speed and ISO yourself. Become familiar with how to set those on your camera. You will want to take a look at your camera's manual to become acquainted.

● Sling the camera over your shoulder and take a walk with me. Not a walk, really, more of a meander. It is the kind of thing you do with a camera. Walk slowly. Follow light or perhaps color or human activity. No agenda except the next frame, out there, waiting to be captured by your camera.

If it turns out to be "the" frame, the keeper, the one you've been waiting for, you don't want to miss it. And you don't want to blow your exposure when you shoot it. The keeper photos are hard to find. Do you really want to blindly trust this machine to get them for you?

No. That's why you have to learn about the basics of exposure. When you get them under your belt, you will be driving the train. The camera will not be driving you.

So—take a deep breath first—move the mode dial off P to M. M stands for "manual," the mode in which you are in control of all of the elements of the exposure—ISO, shutter speed and aperture.

We're outside, so set your ISO to a reasonable number, say 200—even on a relatively cloudy day, ISO ratings around 200 to 400 will give you a good crack at an optimal f-stop/shutter speed combination. Now set your f-stop. Nothing wide open, nothing too closed. A setting of f/5.6 or f/8 would be a reasonable place to start. Now crank your shutter speed dial until the exposure markers line up in the viewfinder. When the hash marks indicate 0, right in the middle, it means the camera meter is judging this combination of settings to be an accurate exposure.

Go click. You've just made an accurate, manual exposure. Say it was 1/125th of a second at f/8. Okay, close the aperture ring down one full stop to f/11. A setting of f/11 provides a smaller opening than f/8, so the shutter speed has to get slower to accommodate the loss of light f/11 represents. It has to get slower by one full shutter speed. In other words, it now needs to be set at 1/60th.

Rome wasn't built in a day, and likewise your familiarity with a digital camera will take time. But these elements of exposure—aperture, shutter speed and ISO—will be with you every step of the way. Experiment! Put an accommodating friend or your ever-patient spouse in front of the lens, and see where these manual combinations lead you. Then compare them to what the P mode would do in the same situation.

There will be overlap—but there will also be differences. When you become familiar with the conditions that produce those differences, you will start to really understand the camera's brain and how it behaves in different lighting situations.

And then you will be able to outthink it.

JOE'S TIP

To make a manual exposure on a digital single-lens reflex (DSLR) camera, you need to know the following things about your model:

CHECKLIST:

❏ **Set the aperture, shutter speed and ISO. In manual mode, which is where you want to play around to learn camera basics, the camera won't help you with this. You control everything—each setting in concert with the other two—through the magic of buttons or dials or menus. You create the right balance—the balance that's right for you.**

❏ **Knowing what a correct exposure looks like before you actually make one is now up to you, but your camera can help you, even in manual mode. There are hash marks in the viewfinder (on the right-hand side or at the bottom edge of the frame, depending upon model) and an indicator that points to under- or over-exposure. If you get that indicator to settle in the middle, the camera is agreeing with you that you've found a good exposure.**

❏ **Just because the camera indicates agreement doesn't mean it's the "right" exposure. The scene may in fact call for under- or over-exposure for effect, and you can program this yourself. Here we have a theme that will be repeated throughout this book: Experiment. Find your own vision.**

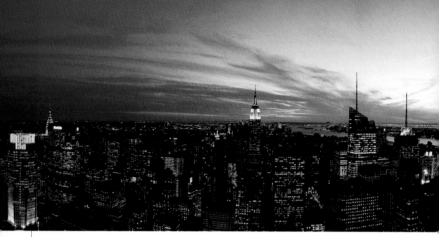

City light in Manhattan, 17MM, 1/5TH AT F/5.6, ISO 200

CITY LIGHT

Imagine the sound of an orchestra warming up: a disconnected, mixed bag of noises. Nothing in sync. Cacophony. The same is true of nighttime cityscapes. Every type of light presents itself, with nothing in arrangement or equal measure. Greens, yellows, reds, all banging into one another like a messy traffic accident. My advice? Put the camera into auto white balance and go for it. If you want to be a bit experimental, shoot some frames while you work your way through the camera's white balance settings. Some bad frames will result, but they will offer valuable information to store away.

Also important: For nightscapes, get set up and ready well before the sun goes down. This way, you'll still have glow and detail in the sky (or rich sunset colors, if you get lucky) just as the city lights start to really shine.

Start snapping too soon, when the sky is still bright, and your shutter speed will be too fast to properly expose the city lights. If you start shooting too late, the night sky will appear black and less than interesting. Postscript: To capture the most city lights, make sure that you try during the workweek, when people are in their offices. On weekends, many windows and buildings are dark.

WINDOW LIGHT

Beautiful. Soft light through a window (or hard light hitting a diffused, gauzy window curtain) is one of the most lovely, forgiving kinds of light for a portrait of a face or a still life of items in a room. It often has a graceful, gradual falloff, letting the highlights rotate into shadows in a slow, easy way. Think of a Vermeer painting or, alternatively, an Irish pub. No hard edges. Round tones and rich details.

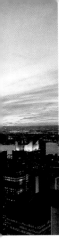

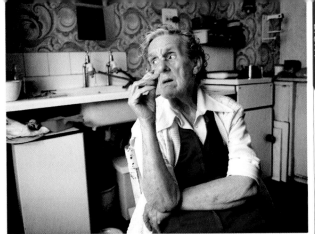

Window light on woman, 35MM, 1/60TH AT F/5.6, ISO 200

MUTED LIGHT

Haze often produces an almost ethereal quality of light. It acts as a gigantic filter that sometimes turns the rising or setting sun into a big soft ball. This can be wonderful because you can expose for the color of the sun and still render detail in the foreground, something not possible when looking into clear, hard, directional sunlight. The lush detail in the foreground of this French countryside is made possible by the hazy conditions, which mute the power of the sun.

Muted, hazy sunrise over the French countryside, 200MM, 1/30TH AT F/4, ISO 100

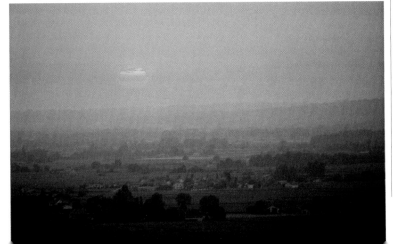

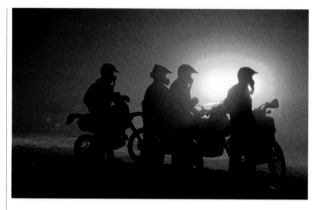

Backlight on Baja bikers, 98MM, 1/15TH AT F/3.5, ISO 400

BACKLIGHT

Backlight means drama, color and silhouettes. Remember to choose interesting, storytelling shapes to silhouette because you have no recognizable details to help out. Backlight can give you a good opportunity to saturate the color of the scene; in other words, underexpose it just a bit. (But be careful! Pointing the camera directly into the source of the backlight will cause it to close the exposure down too severely, and you will end up with a very dark frame with a big spectral highlight in it.) The helmeted Baja bikers, above, backlit by truck headlights in the dust, make distinctive shapes that tell the viewer their story, even though there is no detail in their faces or their bikes.

SIDELIGHT

Light coming from the side generally produces a distinct highlight. Elsewhere in the frame, because of the light's steep angle to the subject, there is shadow. The discrepancy can sometimes be too severe, and the shadow area may require "fill light," such as the kind provided with flash.

Sidelight illuminating a church steeple rising through the trees, Vermont, 200MM, 1/125TH AT F/7.1, ISO 200

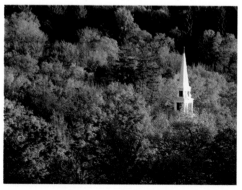

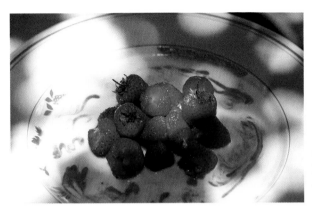

**Dappled light
on strawberries,**
70MM,
1/60TH AT F/2.8,
ISO 100

Other times, this type of light, exposed properly, can be truly dramatic, exciting even. The light on the church steeple, opposite, is coming from camera right, at a steep angle to both the spire and the lens. It highlights one side and drops the other into shadow, which in turn gives the steeple some volume and dimension. The same thing is happening with the trees. There is a wonderful play of highlight and shadow, all produced by sidelight. If this scene were lit by flat, frontal light, you might not even put the camera to your eye.

DAPPLED LIGHT
Dappled light can make you nuts. The beautiful patterns of splashy highlights and instantly dark shadows are often caused by swaying trees or swatches of fast-moving clouds that quickly cover and uncover the sun. In other words, dappling can occur when you think you might be set, and then the light changes. This is a situation in which bracketing is advisable, especially if your subject is static, like mine is above. (Bracketing is all about changing your exposure up and down the scale to make sure that you end up with a properly exposed frame somewhere in the group. After you shoot a photo, try slightly underexposing the same scene and then slightly overexposing a third. One of the exposures is bound to be right.)

Here's the thing: That which drives you to distraction—the constantly changing pattern of light and shadow—is exactly what might produce magic. Splotchy, irregular, unpredictable light can take something pretty ordinary, such as a plate of strawberries, and make it more interesting.

Remember I said light is like language. Used well, it makes for a lively read indeed.

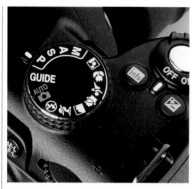

DSLR mode dial set at P,
or program mode

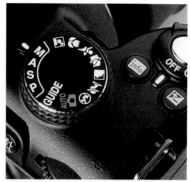

DSLR mode dial set at M,
or manual mode

THE CAMERA'S BRAIN

OR, PICTURES À LA MODE

The camera's exposure meter, at the heart of its computerized brain, has different exposure modes. I've already mentioned a couple of them. Let's take them all in turn, with a bit of review.

PROGRAM MODE

Known as P mode, this is that cautionary mode in which you let the camera do all the work.

Set it on P, and it looks at the scene and then, based on predetermined parameters, selects the aperture–shutter speed combo. As I've said, this is a dangerous way to fly because you are surrendering complete control to a machine. But it's not the worst place to be when you take the camera out of the box and are eager to go make a few pix. Use it initially, while you are getting the feel of the camera in your hands

and seeing the possibilities of whatever lens you may have purchased. Depending on the model, the camera will likely return a pretty good result, most of the time. But it may not represent your vision.

MANUAL MODE

Okay, this is where the rubber meets the road. You've already experimented with this mode and found out how truly easy it is. On M, you drive the train. You select your aperture setting and then match shutter speed to it. I encourage you to experiment here, knowing that smaller aperture openings yield greater across-the-board sharpness, but slower shutter speeds might lead to camera shake and sharpness issues. If you choose a fast shutter speed, you will have to open

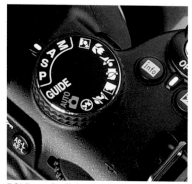

DSLR mode dial set at A,
or aperture priority mode

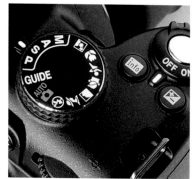

DSLR mode dial set at S,
or shutter priority mode

up the aperture to a wider opening to let in more light. Playing with settings in this way immediately establishes in your head the very direct relationship between shutter speed and f-stop. You're a shooter.

APERTURE PRIORITY MODE

Now that you are getting a bit more comfortable, it's time to become acquainted with a couple of additional exposure modes in which you, the photographer, set one parameter and let the camera automatically react to it.

In aperture priority you select, as you might guess, the lens opening. You might do this for depth-of-field concerns (which we'll address in more detail later). Say you are shooting a big grouping of long-lost cousins at Aunt Tillie's wedding reception. Because your subjects are numerous and thus at different distances to the lens (front row, back row, some kneeling) you want to use a small aperture, perhaps

around f/11, to guarantee that everyone in the frame will be sharp. You set that f-stop, and the camera in A mode will automatically shift the shutter speed. And because it is a high f-stop (big number, small opening) it will be a slower shutter speed.

Then your attention is drawn to the cute flower girl, and you want to snap her portrait. There's only one face in the picture, so no need for f/11. You open up to f/4, a reasonable aperture for a single portrait. Because you're opening up the aperture, you will see the shutter go up the scale and get faster. All well and good.

SHUTTER PRIORITY MODE

Same procedure as above, just in reverse. In S mode, you set the shutter speed and the aperture will slide open or closed, automatically, depending on that shutter speed. Say you are at the rails for the finish of a horse race. Your intent is to freeze the action as the horses come toward the finish line. You need a fast shutter speed, something around 1/1,000th of a second or at least 1/500th. The camera's meter will react by opening up the aperture, or making the hole in the lens bigger, to accommodate the fact that the shutter is moving so quickly.

If your intent, however, is to follow the horses with the camera, keeping the horses sharp while letting the background blur away to indicate how fast they are going, you would do the reverse. Select a shutter speed that can indicate movement (with fast-moving thoroughbreds, this can be 1/60th or slower), and then the meter will react by closing down the aperture to a smaller opening.

HOW TO DETERMINE THE RIGHT EXPOSURE SETTINGS

The camera's pretty darn smart—as you've probably figured out by now. Point those pixels at something, and the camera starts a lightning-fast series of calculations that turns the reality you see through the lens into the amazingly complex bunch of ones and zeroes that constitute a digital image.

But the camera is not, as already discussed, always factoring accurately. That assessment is somewhat unfair, of course. When it makes a "mistake," it is just being its analytical self. Call it a left-brain/right-brain thing. The camera is an engineer, not a poet.

You, on the other hand, have to think with both sides of your brain when you're out there making pictures. You strive for visual poetry, but you have a

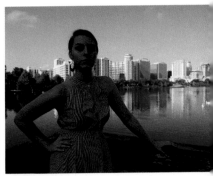

24mm, 1/320th AT F/8, ISO 200

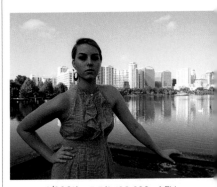

24mm, 1/200th AT F/8, ISO 200, +1 EV

machine in your hands, not a pen and paper. You have to make that machine think like you do.

Above is a good example of the camera returning what it thinks is a completely logical result that is way off base considering where I wanted to go. My portrait subject is the lovely young woman Robin. The camera doesn't know she's a lovely young woman. To the camera, she's just a bunch of

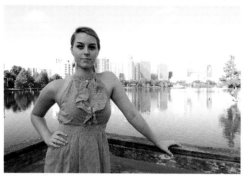

24mm, 1/100th AT F/8, ISO 200, +2 EV

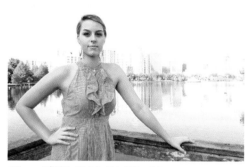

24mm, 1/50th AT F/8, ISO 200, +3 EV

darker pixels. So the first frame at top, left, is, in fact, a good exposure—by the camera's lights. On aperture priority, set at f/8, it measures the sky, the cityscape, the lake and Robin. It makes an exposure based on the overall scene. Bye-bye, Robin!

The camera has not goofed. It did its job well by returning a result that is a "good" exposure across the board, foreground through background. What

it is not aware of is the fact that I wanted to make a picture of Robin.

In the series of exposures on this and the opposite page, I'm going to take control. I will redirect the meter to accommodate my intent. The first exposure is at 1/320th at f/8, with the camera set on aperture priority. I used this mode because I wanted to set a lens opening that would render Robin sharply but also have reasonable sharpness extending out to the scene behind her. The shutter speed reacts to the scene brightness by setting itself at 1/320th.

In straight-up aperture priority mode, I can't make the camera see any differently than this. Remember I said that as I adjust my f-stop, the camera will shift the shutter speed accordingly? The camera strives to return the same overall exposure value relative to what it sees. So here, if I shifted one f-stop more open, to f/5.6, would the scene get brighter?

No. The meter would then move the speed to 1/640th, a shutter that is twice as fast, reacting to the fact that I just let in twice as much light through the lens opening.

So, to make this brighter and see Robin, do I have to go to manual? That

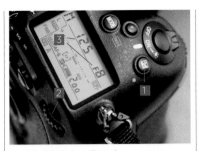

On this DSLR, to adjust the exposure value compensation, you would press the EV button [1] to activate while turning the adjustment wheel [2] to set the value to plus or minus. The LCD readout [3] shows your setting.

would be a solution, for sure. I could switch to M mode and start pushing and pulling f-stops and shutter speeds until I got where I wanted to go. But I can make adjustments, right here in aperture priority mode, using exposure value compensation.

The exposure compensation, or EV control, is, on most digital cameras, a small button usually located near the shutter button. Small button, big impact. When I depress this button, the camera allows me to adjust the existing exposure it has sorted out. I can make it brighter (plus EV) or darker (minus EV). These moves correspond to aperture adjustments or shutter adjustments, depending on which mode I am in.

For Robin's picture, I know I need to make things brighter. So I punch the EV button and program in "plus one stop." You can see the result on page 34. She gets brighter—not enough, but a bit.

(Funny, she gets brighter by about one stop.)

That means I redirected the camera meter to overexpose one full stop of light. Because I am in aperture priority mode, and I have designated my aperture of choice, the shutter becomes the slider, or variable. It now pulls in at 1/200th of a second, slower than the original 1/320th, thus letting light hit the sensor for a longer duration.

Okay, more work to do. Hit the EV button again, this time going to plus two EV. Now the shutter speed floats to 1/100th. Slower still. Robin gets brighter. What also gets brighter? The background. We are, in full-stop increments of light, saying goodbye to the city of Orlando.

To get Robin fully up to speed in terms of exposure, once again I hit the EV button, programming plus three EV. Shutter is now 1/50th. She is good to go exposure-wise. The city and background are blown out.

In shutter priority mode, the same process occurs, but the variable is the f-stop. Each "plus one" move on the EV dial will result in the f-stop going from f/8 to f/5.6 to f/4 to f/2.8. The shutter, prioritized in this mode, stays where you put it.

The camera's brain fires in consistent fashion. What is not consistent, of course, is the world it encounters, a world full of backlight, sidelight, hard light, shadows and drama. Our heads, hearts and eyes have to show it the way. And, once you get proficient at pushing these buttons and moving these dials, the camera will follow.

SHOOTING WITH LOW LIGHT

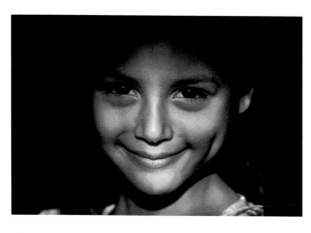

Young girl under low light, 50MM, 1/125TH AT F/2.8, ISO 100

The roots of the word photography are from the Greek: photo, meaning "light," and graphein, meaning "to write." To write with light. Very expressive, those Greeks.

● So what do you do when there is hardly any light? Put down your pencil, close your notebook (the camera) and go home? I would caution against that. Those who go home early lose.

Stay for the darkness. The less light there is, the more shadows there are. The more shadows, the more intrigue and mystery. Low light imparts a softness that fades to black in the most magical of ways. This is where the arts of photography and painting converge. This is where you, the shooter, are like a hunter in a quiet forest. There is simplicity of form and content. You can hear yourself breathe behind the

lens. As opposed to the carnival at high noon—a riot of garish color, abundant light, odd smells and loud sounds—there is a quietude in low light, a peace. You have to find it. This requires patience . . . and skill. At these low-light hours of the day, predawn or twilight, light is like a whisper.

Listen.

Because you have a bunch of plastic, glass and wiring in your hands to see with—and not just your enormously adaptive eyes that record all this dimness with relative ease—there are, of course, techniques you should observe when shooting in low light. Low light means slow shutter speeds. As we have discussed, the slower, or longer, the shutter speed, the more light is allowed to pass through the lens and hit the chip. It's like opening a window to let in some fresh air: The longer you have it open, the more fresh air comes in. Same with a camera and a lens. Low light demands that you open that gate to the sensor for longer and longer periods of time—maybe 1/8th of a second, or even 1/4th. That doesn't seem all that long, but when you are trying to hold a camera steady, it's an eternity.

For most people, especially those just coming out of the blocks with a digital camera, slow shutter speeds are killers. They lead to blurry pictures and disappointment. Disappointment leads to disillusionment and discouragement, which leads to putting the camera back in the box. Which leads to clicking on-line to eBay. OUT-OF-FOCUS CAMERA FOR SALE! CHEAP!

Don't do it. Shooting in low light requires special skills, but it has very special rewards. Read on, and let's talk.

YOUR CAMERA AND LOW LIGHT

Does your camera like low light? Not really. Of course, I've been talking throughout this section about the camera being a machine and not knowing or liking much of anything. But low light presents it with a challenge. After all, a camera is designed to record light, so as you might imagine, it can get a little balky when confronted with minimal amounts of it. There are things it will do, and things you should do to compensate.

Work on a tripod. The three-legged beast, as vexing as it is to tote around, will save your neck in low light. As the light level dives, your shutter speeds slow down. There comes a point at which prudence dictates the use of a tripod, even for experienced, seasoned shooters, who may have developed deft camera-holding techniques over the years.

Tripods come in all sizes. A rule of thumb: The longer and heavier the lens-camera combo, the sturdier the tripod needs to be. There is no sense mounting a 600mm lens on the handy-dandy, cheapo rig the salesman talked you into, the one with the swizzle sticks for legs and the ball head that wouldn't effectively stabilize a cup of coffee, much less long glass. Get a brand-name, sturdy tripod. It doesn't have to be a monster, just something that isn't going to tip over in the first stiff breeze.

What to do if there is no tripod at hand? Improvise! Crouch down. Sacrifice a smidge of the perfect angle you had and rest your elbows on your knees. Find a wall to lean against or a telephone pole to wrap yourself around. Do you have a jacket or a hoodie? Take it off and make a beanbag out of it, and then nestle the camera down on that. Look around: There's bound to be something you can prop the camera on that will help you keep this picture you desperately want sharp.

Oh, and when you are in improv, seat-of-the-pants mode, shoot lots of frames. Lots—it will improve your odds.

If the going gets interminably slow, and that shutter of yours is open long enough to play a game of Risk, then it might be time for a cable release. This small but potentially crucial piece of

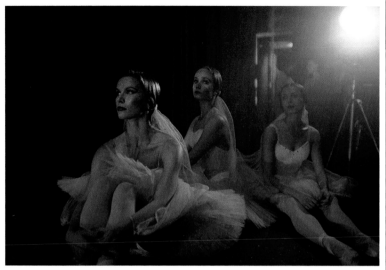

Ballet dancers at rest illuminated by low, blue light, 35MM, 1/30TH AT F/2.8, ISO 100

gear is simply a plunger that connects to the shutter and allows you to fire the camera without actually touching it. In this digital age, most cable releases are electronic rather than the older push-plunger (squeeze) types (which still exist and interface with certain film cameras, especially larger format ones). The new breed of cable release is simply a button attached to a cord that hooks up to the camera.

There are simple cable releases and fancy ones. Any good camera system has its own dedicated, proprietary type of release that plugs into its particular electronic interface, located on the camera body, and runs from there through a length of electrical cord to a button you can press. The higher-end systems feature timers that will give you control of extremely long exposures and control over when those exposures will occur. Others are really simple: You push the button, the camera fires. (There are also camera models out there that have, as an additional piece of equipment, a wireless trigger that allows you to fire the camera as long as you are within a few feet of it.)

Whatever the mechanism, a cable release allows the camera to make an exposure without you touching it—which is the point. Even when you have your camera mounted on a tripod, simply pushing the shutter button during an extremely long exposure might cause problems. Depending on

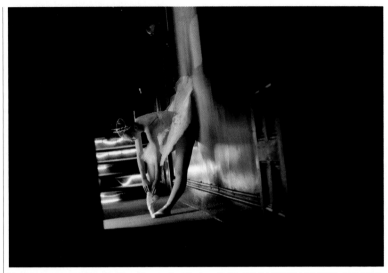

Ballet dancer waiting in the wings, shot in low light, 70MM, 1/30TH AT F/2.8, ISO 6400

how much coffee you've had that day, you could shake the whole rig and wind up with a blurry photo.

These are important things to be concerned about when you backstop yourself during times of low light. While you are being sensible and doing what you can to take the best possible picture, what is the camera doing?

LOW-LIGHT SETTINGS

Whether there's an abundance of light or very little, the camera continues being its robotic self—which is not necessarily a bad thing. There are a number of ways it reacts to dark conditions, and you should familiarize yourself with them.

If you are in P mode, or a completely auto type of exposure, the camera will be setting the f-stop–shutter speed combo for you. If it gets to a point where it thinks you are in danger of shooting a blurry photo, it will warn you. (This generally occurs when it drifts below 1/60th of a second.) Depending on the camera model, you might get a beep, or even a little hand symbol waving at you, indicating that the camera thinks your hand-holding technique isn't worth spit.

If you are in aperture or shutter priority exposure mode, you will be responsible for setting, or programming, either the shutter speed or f-stop. In aperture mode, push your f-stop to its widest opening, in hopes that the shutter speed will stay in an area you feel comfortable handling. In shutter mode, you will have to keep slowing down your shutter to accommodate low-light conditions and the speed of your lens. If it is a slow lens, an f/4 to f/5.6, for example, you will be forced to keep your shutter open longer than you would if your lens were faster, such as an f/2.8.

You can make adjustments to the camera's settings that will enable it to deal with low light, the major one being its ISO. If you've been reading through the book from page 1, you know that ISO governs the speed at which the sensor will accept and react to light. For low light, expect to push your ISO numbers all the way up there toward 1600, 3200 or even (gasp!) 6400.

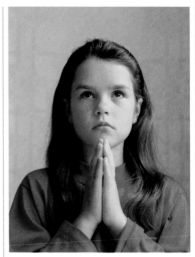

Young girl lit by soft, low light,
150MM, 1/100TH AT F/5.6, ISO 100

These superhigh ISO ratings will get you a picture, but boy will you pay a price, at least in the middle-of-the-road type of digital camera. High ISOs tend to result in digital "noise," or what we used to call "grain" in film. A noisy picture generally lacks contrast and detail, and printing such a frame is a nightmare. (The flagship digital cameras can handle high ISOs really well, by the way. This performance factor is one reason pros use them and why they cost a boatload of dough. Cheaper or even moderately priced cameras don't perform as effectively at these accelerated ISOs.)

Many digital cameras come equipped with a feature that can take your mind off constantly fiddling with your ISO number in response to changes in light. Predictably, it's called Auto ISO. This mode allows the camera to shift ISO all on its own. I always rail about surrendering such a crucial decision to the camera, but I've seen this one perform and, frankly, it's a pretty useful feature of the powerful new digital machines we make pictures with. You can set parameters in this mode so that it doesn't run amok. It stays within the limits you are comfortable with.

Practice, and play with the various bells and whistles on your digital camera. The more you practice and refer to your own notes on the picture-making process, the easier shooting with your camera becomes. Push it, pull it, adjust it. Get to know the soul of the digital machine.

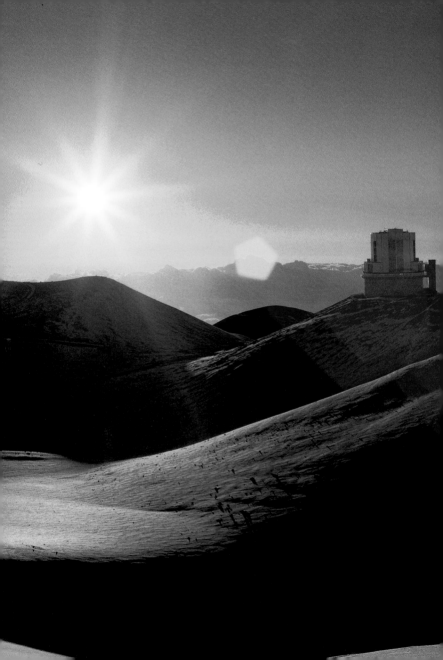

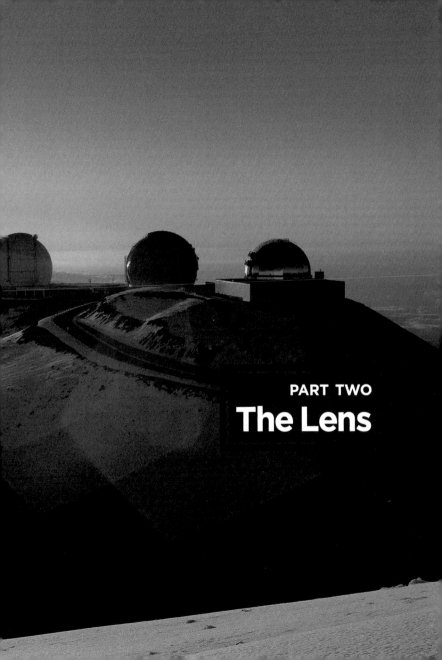

PART TWO
The Lens

The lens is the eye of the camera. Yet, the human eye is a tough act to follow. It is audacious, ridiculous even, to think that a collection of glass elements, coatings, metal rings and aperture blades could substitute for the incredibly supple instrument that supplies us with all of the visual information we will receive in our lifetimes.

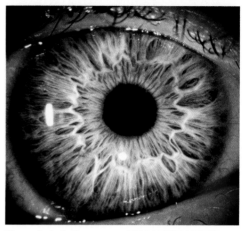

Macro shot of a human eye, 105MM, 1/60TH AT F/16,

● The human eye is nothing short of amazing. It has mechanics, sensitivity and wiring that even the best of digital cameras can only dream about. Linking with the brain, the eye can sweep a dark alley, pulling out detail from the dimmest corners and depths, and then swing out to a brightly lit street scene exploding with highlights and backlights, making the adjustment to those extremes in nanoseconds. Sensitive and responsive, it deals with and even thrives in a world of darks, lights, exuberant colors and subtle monochromes.

The lens on a digital camera, directed by the eye of the photog, embraces all that cool-looking stuff out there, too. Yet it funnels it, not to the supercomputer known as the human brain, but to a very limited sensor, or chip. Think of taking a gallon jug of milk and trying to pour it into an eight-ounce glass. That's kind of what the lens is doing. Digital cameras, when faced with the amazing extremes of color and light in the world, shrug. They can't possibly cope with all of it. TMI—too much information—big time.

The human eye can effectively see detail in dark, dark shadows, and bright, bright highlights. This spectrum from darks to lights is referred to as dynamic range. Digital cameras can't handle nearly the dynamic range of the human eye. Think of it this way: The diaphragm of the lens opens and closes in increments, called f-stops. The eye can see and process the equivalent of about 12 to 14 f-stops of light, which is a vast range. The fanciest digital camera out there can only handle about 5 stops. So, how do you make your lens and camera behave even just a bit more like your eye and brain?

Use lenses well. Understand what they do and how they function. Handle and hold them properly. Make sure the lens you choose is the right tool for that job or that moment. The lens is your point of view, your window to the world or the mirror you use to look at your own life and the lives of those around you. If you can understand how to choose and use lenses well, you have a crack at making this machine in your hands look at things the way your eye does.

The lens you use defines how and what you see, and photography is all about seeing.

WHAT, AGAIN, IS APERTURE?

Aperture, as I've mentioned, is a hole in your lens through which light travels. Bigger hole, more light. Smaller hole, less light. In this age of fancy-pants digital cameras that have a gazillion menu items and just about cook your breakfast for you, that description sounds absurdly simple, prehistoric even.

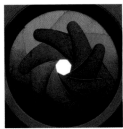

Lens aperture closed down to f/16

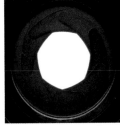

Lens aperture opened up to f/4

But at the end of the day, in simplest terms, that's the aperture. It is somewhat refreshing to see that this crucial element of the photographic process has not really changed much over the years. The hole, as I indicated, can range from big, which is often referred to in photo lingo as "wide open," to small, referred to as "closed down." It is adjustable along the way from big to small in clicks, or f-stops.

Sounds simple—and it is. But, as with all things photographic, there are other issues that present themselves with every click of an f-stop. F-stops can be adjusted manually, if you have the camera set in manual mode. Or if you're using that popular exposure mode known as aperture priority, you, the photographer, designate the f-stop you wish to work at, and the camera automatically shifts the shutter speed to keep exposure pace with whatever f-stop you've choosen.

It's important to remember that the higher your f-stop number, the smaller the opening in the lens and the less light you are allowing to transit the lens to the sensor. The lower the number, the bigger the opening—meaning lots of light is pouring onto the sensor. Hence, at f/16 (high number), your

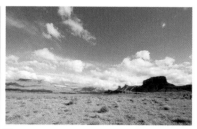
19mm

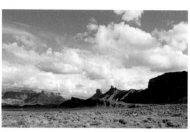
35mm

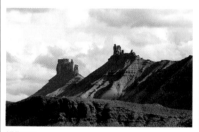
135mm

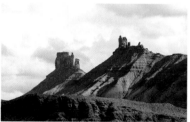
150mm

hole in the lens is quite small. At f/2.8 (low number), it is very large. Welcome to the mildly illogical world of picture-taking.

As I mentioned previously, each full f-stop click along the way represents either twice as much or half as much light as the previous f-stop, depending on which direction you are heading. So—stick with me here—when you go from f/16 to f/11, you are doubling your light. Click from f/11 to f/8 and again you are doubling the amount of light. Clicking from a higher to a lower number is referred to as "opening up" the lens, or the f-stop. Moving in the other direction, say from f/4 to f/5.6, halves the light with each full f-stop click. This is called "closing down" the lens or f-stop.

The best way to get your head around all of this talk of f-stops and aperture is to point your camera at a simple nondescript subject, such as an evenly lit wall. Fill the frame with the wall, and click up and down through the f-stop range. You will get a feel for how aperture behaves and how much light there is in one f-stop.

FIELD OF VIEW

When I say "field of view," I am referring to what you see through the lens. Shorter, wide lenses embrace the whole scene, while longer lenses parcel it out in smaller bits. Lenses are referred to by numbers, such as 70mm or 200mm, that are based upon the lens's focal length, which is the distance from point of focus in

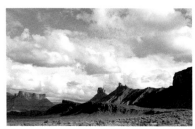

50mm

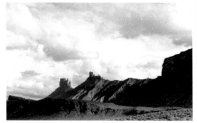

70mm

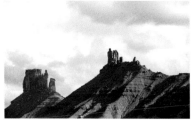

200mm

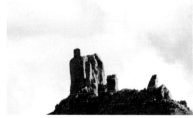

600mm

the center of the lens to the sensor, or chip. (This used to be called a film plane, back when we ran rolls of acetate through the backs of cameras.)

Pretty dry stuff, huh? But here's the thing: Lenses are very exciting. Lenses provide the size of the window our cameras use to peer at the world. Get a group of photogs together talking tech, and lenses invariably come up. "You get that new 300 f/2.8? Sweet!" Or, "How about that 14? Gorgeous!"

Superlatives fly around like crazy. *Sweet, smooth, incredible, sharp, beautiful, fast, great, super*—you might think those photogs are talking about a fashion model driving a Ferrari. No, nothing that exotic or scintillating. Just some glass stuffed into a metal tube

that we look through. But the reasons chests heave, passions ignite and words gush is that the lens is incredibly important to what photographers do; it defines what we see.

Take a look at the pictures above, all shot from the same vantage point, with the same camera and the same camera settings. The choice of lens allows you to take a trip without moving. You throw the door wide open to the full magnificence of mountains, clouds and sky with a 19mm, and then you slowly close in while traveling through a series of lenses all the way to a 600mm, which yields a very narrow slice of the scene. The overall result? Different pictures emphasizing different elements and telling very different stories.

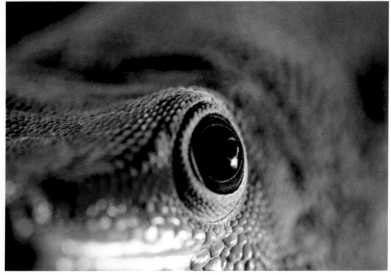

Macro shot of a reptile with limited depth of field, 300mm, 1/125th at f/11, ISO 100

[DEPTH OF FIELD]

● As with aperture, depth of field, or DOF, is, at its core, a very simple thing. DOF refers to what is sharp in the picture. Now, there's critically sharp and acceptably sharp—and there's a crucial difference between the two. Critical sharpness should be achieved on the key element of your picture. What is around that absolutely sharp point should be acceptably sharp, or within depth of field. DOF generally divides itself this way: One-third of it leads up to the point of critical sharpness, and two-thirds leads away from it. In other words, there is more sharpness in the background than the foreground.

Do an eyeball exercise in DOF. Focus on an object very close to you. You should be vaguely aware that objects in the distance are blurry. Now shift your eyes to the blurry background material. This now gets sharp, while your original foreground point of focus gets fuzzy. It's impossible to focus on both subjects simultaneously.

Even the eye can't do it, though sometimes we think it can because the eye-brain combo is so fast and seamless while it makes adjustments.

You've just done a DOF exercise, using your eye. A camera does the same thing: Put something close to the lens, focus on it and the background goes soft, or out of focus. Push the focus ring past that close object, and select a focal point in the background. The object in front of the lens that you originally focused on is now an out-of-focus

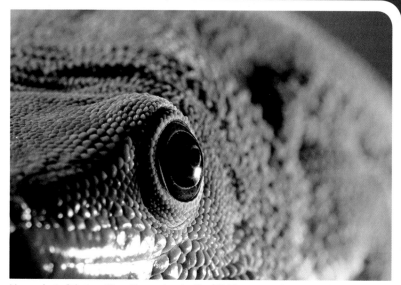

Macro shot of that reptile with greater depth of field, 300MM, 1/125TH AT F/32, ISO 100

blob. Depth of field at work.

Your eye-brain team operates automatically and at such lightning speed that you're not really aware of the constantly changing pattern of what's in focus and what's out. This process is instinctive, just part of the day. But you must be aware of DOF when you are shooting pictures. As opposed to just letting your eyeballs do their thing, you can actually step in to manage and direct the camera to produce greater or shallower depth of field.

Remember when an

DO THIS FIRST

When you're looking to gauge your depth of field, choose an appropriate aperture before shooting. Remember that there are three principal things to pay attention to: how long the lens is, the size of the aperture and how close you are to the subject. The longer the lens, and the closer you are to the subject, the shorter the DOF. If you want to compensate and get greater depth of field in such a situation, then you have to close down your aperture.

object really close to the lens was sharp and pretty much everything else was a blur? Keep that quickie lesson in mind. The closer the subject, the shallower the depth of field. In other words, the range or distance between things that are sharp to the things that aren't gets much shorter. By contrast,

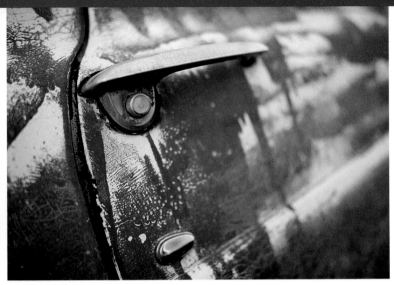

Car door with shallower depth of field, 24MM, 1/2,500TH AT F/1.4, ISO 200

"The key element in your picture should be critically sharp. What is around that element should be acceptably sharp."

if your subject is in the middle distance or far away—in other words, not particularly close to the lens—your depth of field gets much greater.

How much? Tough to say because DOF is dependent on another crucial factor, and that is aperture. Remember I said there are other issues besides exposure control that moving the f-stop ring will affect? DOF is the big one.

The smaller your f-stop (high number), the greater the depth of field. At wider aperture settings, the depth of field gets very limited.

Lens choice affects DOF as well. The longer the lens, the shorter the depth of field. Wider glass will stretch out depth of field. For example, a 20mm lens at f/22 will yield tremendous DOF, but a 300mm lens at f/4 will have relatively shallow DOF.

That's a lot of numbers, right? Sounds like math, not picture-taking. So what do they mean to you in the field?

A lot . . . and nothing. Here's the thing: Picture-taking requires practice. Shoot, and shoot again, and again. The numbers, laborious to figure out at first, give way to

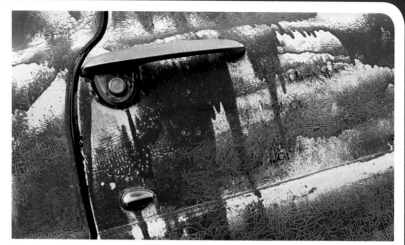

Car door with greater depth of field, 24MM, 1/50TH AT F/11, ISO 200

intuition—so much so that when you hunker down on the ground to shoot the foreground clump of daisies with the purple mountains majesty in the distance, you instinctively move your f-stop into the higher numbers to get greater depth of field. You remember the one-third/two-thirds rule of DOF, so you know a bit of the foreground grass will get sharper, but the real benefit is extending the sharpness into the background. Because of your quick, simple f-stop adjustment, the distant mountains are discernible, and not just vague, out-of-focus lumps.

Likewise, when you shoot a portrait of your kid at the local street fair, and there are wires, cords, clowns, pedestrians and other distracting junk in the background, you push the camera in closer and open the f-stop to around f/2.8 or f/4. Your child stays sharp, and the background softens up but still retains the sense of a busy celebration.

There's lots to talk about with depth of field. It's, well, deep.

JOE'S TIP

Depth of field is pretty simple once you get used to it. These things will become instinctive, but for now, commit them to memory if you can, or make a crib sheet of this checklist:

CHECKLIST:

❐ The closer you are to your subject, the shallower the DOF (less of your image is in focus).

❐ To shoot a picture with the shallowest DOF, set your aperture as wide as possible, such as f/1.4, 2.8 or 3.5.

❐ The farther you are from your subject, the greater the DOF (more of your image is in focus).

❐ To shoot a picture with the greatest DOF, set your aperture as small as possible, such as f/16, 22 or 32.

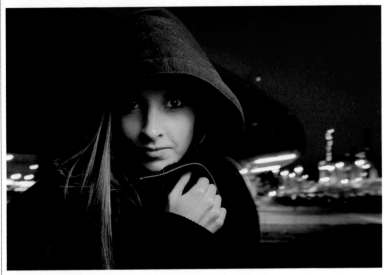

Portrait shot with a wide lens, 24MM, 0.6 SEC. AT F/2.8, ISO 400

It's a wide, wild, woolly, wacky, wonderful world out there. But let's just stick with wide for now. Wide-angle lenses, or wide glass as they are known, give you the ability to include in a picture elements we are only somewhat aware of when we are staring straight ahead at a scene. These elements live on the edges of our eyesight, in peripheral vision.

● Whereas a telephoto lens, which we will learn about later, allows us to eliminate distance and zoom in on a subject, a wide-angle lens does pretty much the opposite: It throws its arms out to the sides and embraces an entire scene. A good wide-angle lens is a must for any shooter's equipment bag. It is an effective, necessary tool for setting a scene, snapping a group portrait, shooting in tight quarters or doing landscape photography and environmental portraiture. What wide glass does is establish context. It answers questions. What does the scene look like? How far away is it? How close is that thing to the other thing?

Wide glass tells stories. Consider for a moment a tight portrait shot with a longish lens. Done well, this portrait can tell you a bit about the subject's life, to be sure. The lines on a face may speak volumes. The eyes might be weary or bright. The roughness of skin might imply a hard life. You can tell a lot from the close look a telephoto creates. But you can't tell where the subject is or what the subject is doing.

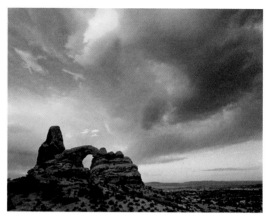

Moab, Utah, 17MM, 1/160TH AT F/8, ISO 200

Wide lenses locate people and places. They show relationships. Switch from a long lens to a wide lens, and a face becomes a face in a place. There's more information. You give your viewer other things to chew on, more to think about. Pulling back from a tight view to a wide view allows the shooter to bring in items the viewer will tune in to. Business suit, overalls, military uniform? Bank lobby, fishing dock, fourth-grade classroom? Showing context can often complete the story you began to tell when you became intrigued with someone's face.

Wide lenses are the answer for landscapes. They are essential for showing the depth and breadth of either the natural or man-made world. I wouldn't tackle either the canyons of Manhattan or those of Arizona without one. One workhorse wide-angle zoom that is always in my bag is the 24–70mm. It is just wide enough to grab very horizontal scenes, and it gives me room to push in closer and distill things a bit. It's very handy as a walk-around lens.

I view a 24mm lens as civilized, controlled. Just wide enough, thank you. Proper. Fairly easy to control. But, have you ever been at an ice cream parlor and ordered a vanilla cone with one scoop, and the guy next to you is slurping the double chocolate banana whammy with the extra whipped cream and an avalanche of cherries? You look on with longing. I believe the expression is "wistful."

That's how I feel about serious wide-angle lenses. A 24mm or so will suffice, but the real tasty adventure of wide glass is in the smaller numbers, down around 20, 18, 16 and (yikes!) even 14mm. There are a multitude of wide-angle zoom lenses that traffic in these numbers; such ranges as 14–24 and 16–35 are commonly available.

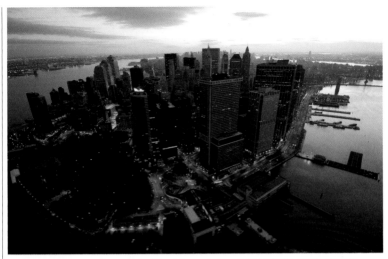

Lower Manhattan at dawn shot with wide-angle lens, 18MM, 1/10TH AT F/4, ISO 400

These smaller numbers get you a really wide view of the world.

Taking a wide view is wonderful, but, as with any adventure, there can be pitfalls. The biggest, to my mind, is the sheer childlike enthusiasm shooters inevitably succumb to when they first get one of these puppies in their hands. "This is really wide! Cool! I can get *everything* in my picture!"

Yes, you can. And, as I have cautioned already and will again, you can easily get nothing in your picture. Really wide glass should come packaged with hazard warnings, as far as I'm concerned. First-timers with wide-angle fever tend to show lots of pictures that have subjects of interest that are very, very tiny and in the back of the frame. Up front is a really, really

wide expanse of . . . emptiness.

Be careful of introducing your viewers to a vast void in the foreground of your picture. You are asking them, quite frankly, to work too hard to involve themselves in a scene that you thought was so magnificent, you just had to squeeze all of it into one picture. The human eye is easily bored. Just think of how many pictures are being made out there, all of them screaming for attention. It becomes visual white noise, and the eye goes to sleep. It needs something that causes it to snap to attention. If your picture can do that, you win.

When working wide glass, a great way to create interest is to anchor the foreground of the photograph. Out there in the wild, try to find elements close in that complement the scene, give good information, provide compositional pizzazz and add color. *And then put these things in the foreground.* A blasted tree, a marvelously intricate rock formation or even a single dandelion, placed strategically in close to the lens, can make or break a landscape. In the big city, a stoplight, a lone pedestrian or a colorful awning can humanize and scale the concrete jungle. Compose your overall scene so that these foreground elements spark interest, captivate your viewers and stimulate a visual journey through the photo. In other words, you have to find this thing, this anchor, and once you do, you must handle it well in the frame. For a story on the long history of London's River Thames, I used a wide lens to frame the scene, but made sure there was foreground interest by showing the ancient artifacts treasure hunters find in the river. In the photograph at right, we see various elements working together to tell the river's tale.

When you're using wide glass, stay active; a wide picture shot from eye level and middle distance can be a real yawner—a one-way ticket to Boringville. If you want to shoot that flower, get down there

with it. Push the wide-angle lens in close. (Remember to click to a high f-stop to close down your aperture. You most likely want a lot of DOF in a photo like this.)

Climb something! Find an elevated view that gets you a better look at that red rock formation you wish to put in the foreground.

Get off the beaten track! Wander!

The wide-angle lens covers a lot of ground. So must you.

Artifacts from the River Thames shot with wide-angle lens, 24MM, 1/30TH AT F/11, ISO 64

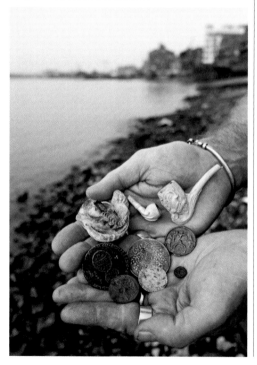

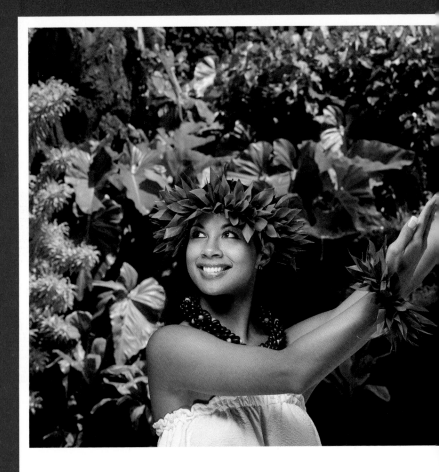

[PORTRAITS AND DOF]

"*In portraiture, most times, you strive for selective sharpness. What's sharp and what's not send a powerful message: 'Look here! Not there!'*"

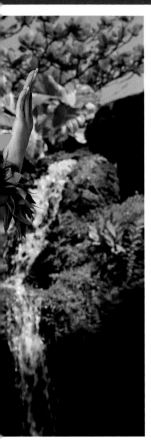

Hawaiian dancer,
86MM, 1/125TH
AT F/14, ISO 100

● There are lots of buttons, dials, clicks and wheels on today's versatile and powerful digital picture-making machines. They all have their own functions and sets of numbers: 1/125th! Half a stop! Plus one EV! And f/6.3! Different from f/3.5!

It would be easy to face this onslaught of calculations and just surrender. Give up, dial the camera back to P and let it do the math. This is completely understandable. Picture-taking is supposed to be great, passionate fun. Factoring, say, exposure relative to DOF in a backlit situation can be pretty tiresome. But here's the thing: Every single one of those buttons and numbers means something to your photograph. And although they are just numbers, they have enormous impact on the aesthetic of the picture, determining whether it's any good or not.

Let's take a look at a couple of portraits to see if depth of field has anything to do with whether each image works or not. I made the first picture of this lovely Hawaiian dancer with a lens set at 86mm, at 1/125th of a second at f/14. It is a solid exposure across the board. The foreground and background are well exposed; the sky is a rich blue. From a technical standpoint, I did well. But

DO THIS FIRST

Be aware of how much DOF you have in your image and, equally important, what is contributing to that DOF and what can be adjusted. Do you have too much or too little for the desired effect? If so, focus on the three things that govern the outcome: length of lens, size of aperture and closeness of the camera to the subject. If you're not where you want to be, change lenses, adjust your aperture or move up or back.

is it successful creatively? Hmmm . . .

It's not my favorite frame, to be sure. One of the problems is the choice of f/14 and its resultant huge depth of field. Front to back, there is tremendous detail and sharpness, and this works against the success of the photo.

Hey, wait a minute! I thought pictures were

supposed to be sharp! True enough, but in portraiture, most times, you strive for selective sharpness. What's sharp and what's not send a powerful message to the viewer. You are saying "Look here! Not there!" You drive attention to your subject's eyes and face. The rest of the frame is supporting cast. Those other elements contribute information and are the staging. They are not supposed to overwhelm.

In the 86mm shot on page 56, those elements do overwhelm by virtue of their dead-bang crispness. You can barely discern where the leafy headdress the dancer is wearing stops and the tree behind her starts. She looks like she's standing in front of that big plant in *Little Shop of Horrors,* and that sucker is about to swallow her.

But in the midst of this relative failure (not *total* failure—maybe the Maui Chamber of Commerce would like this for a brochure), I did notice something: The dancer had a luminous smile and a real twinkle in her eyes. Immediately, I knew that's where I wanted to go. I needed to isolate those elements.

That would be tough to do with this midrange lens and all those f-stops. So I switched up and went telephoto, to 200mm. Remember I said that telephotos reach in to parcel out a scene? They get the details of the face—and little else—used close in this way. Near the greenery was a pool with a waterfall, so I asked the dancer to get in the water, and I got wet, too, lowering the lens right at water level. The waterfall splashes directly behind her, but it is just lively texture and patterns. The focus is on her face, specifically her eyes, which are sparkling.

Only the face is sharp because I shot the lens at f/2, as wide open as possible: Small number, big hole in the lens. Minimal depth of field— razor thin, in fact. You still know you are in the islands, with the leaves and the water. And you are engaged by her wonderful expression and directness. You look nowhere else because there's just the hint of atmosphere, not a cacophony of it, screaming for attention.

All those numbers add up.

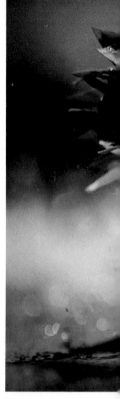

Hawaiian dancer, 200mm, 1/5,000TH AT F/2, ISO 100

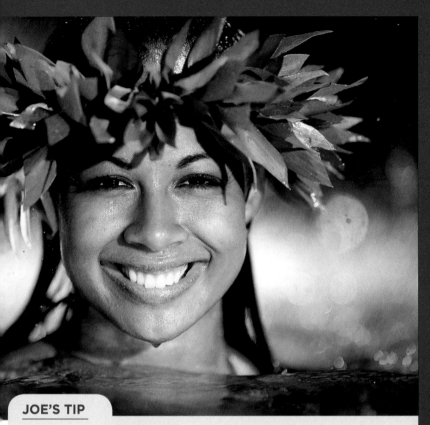

JOE'S TIP

When you are taking this kind of portrait, and you decide that shallower DOF is what you want, remember the following:

CHECKLIST:

❏ Visualize the portrait. Decide what crucial elements you want sharp. People ask me all the time, "What's the key thing to make sharp?" My answer, when dealing with portraits, is, "The near eye." This doesn't matter so much with the dancer here—both eyes are in the same plane of focus—but it has proved a useful strategy for me over the years.

You'll come up with your own rules of thumb, and I hope some of them are derived from these pages. As you go forward and gain experience, trust them. Rely on them. Lean on them. They will be the foundation for the shooter you become.

❏ Open up your aperture as far as you can, to f/1.4, f/2.0 or f/2.8.

❏ If you want truly minimal depth of field, go with a longer lens and fill the frame with your subject: Push the lens in close.

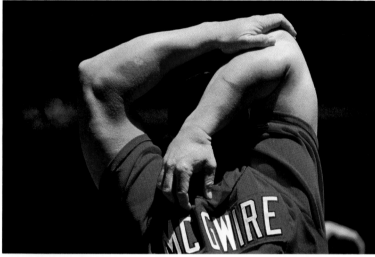

Mark McGwire, 200mm, 1/250TH AT F/8, ISO 100

One thing the human eye cannot do is get bigger. It cannot magnify objects or go telephoto all on its own. This is one huge, cool thing the right camera-lens combo can do that the eye cannot do. As you stand on the sidelines of a football game watching with your naked peepers, unless the action comes in your direction, the scrum out there on the field is going to be occurring roughly in the same register and dimension all day long. You can't enter the action unless you want to get trampled by huge, fast-moving players wearing the equivalent of gladiators' armor. And your eyes simply can't grow legs on their own and trot out for a closer look.

● With a telephoto lens, however, you can do just that—get your eyes on the field. Via the mechanics of a telephoto lens, you can "fill the frame" with magnified action that your sideline-bound eyeballs perceive as only a small part of a generally observed scene. Instead of just seeing a messy collection of well-muscled combatants flinging one another about, with a good telephoto you are right there, in the mix of the blood and sweat, the grunting, the heaving—the emotions. Think of it as a transporter that just beamed your point of view right into the middle of the huddle.

(While we're talking sidelines,

here's a sideline comment about shooting action with a telephoto: Keep your wits about you. If those behemoths out there suddenly get very, very large in the frame, they are coming toward you, probably very rapidly. You can dive so far into a telephoto that you lose a sense of where you are. Giddy with excitement at the play coming your way, you're recording popped eyes, flared nostrils and flying sweat. You're there! So close you can see the laces on the old pigskin! And that's your last conscious thought as the person carrying aforementioned pigskin runs right over you and your new, remarkable telephoto lens. Cleat marks on the front element of a lens are not recommended, unless you're striving for a special effect.)

Telephoto lenses, simply put, bring us close to what we are observing from afar. Referred to as "long" lenses or "long glass," telephotos are important tools when a situation demands to be rendered with magnification and impact. Imagine you're at your kid's soccer game and she scores the winning goal. You shoot it with a 50mm normal lens. Then you have to keep explaining to anyone looking at the picture (and proud parent that you are, that would be everyone you meet) that there's Susie, right there, kicking the ball. You need to explain, see, because little Susie is about 7 or 8 of the 30 million pixels churned out by your fancy digital camera, which means the ball she's kicking is about 2 pixels big.

Microscopic, in other words. Inconsequential. This kind of situation is where a telephoto rules. With a long lens, as you develop the skills of holding it properly and instinctively tracking action (no silver bullet stuff here, just practice—and a few tips later in this book, beginning on page 67), you would be right on Susie, following her path down the field as she avoids defenders, kicks the game-winner and jumps for joy when her teammates mob her. The telephoto lens tells that kind of story. With the magic of magnification, you are right there with little Susie, recording a moment she will remember forever, at least partly because Mom or Dad shot it well.

HOW TO SHOOT WITH A TELEPHOTO
So, how do you "shoot it well" with a telephoto lens? The first thing to do is choose wisely. Big is good, with telephotos, but bigger, or really, really big is not necessarily best. Consider what you like to shoot. Is it in fact soccer or other sports? Or is it landscapes and wildlife? Or are you a street shooter who travels and wants to record the interesting faces of a foreign (or familiar) culture naturally, without being intrusive? All of these might call for a different focal length of lens.

After 30 years in the field, I can say with assurance that one of the most useful (and used) lenses I tote is a 70–200mm telephoto. The millimeter range on this lens is very versatile, and it is capable of embracing many of the diverse situations all photographers

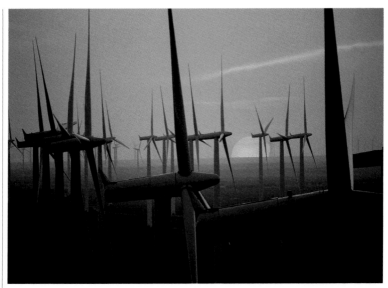

Wind farm, 400MM, 1/1,600TH AT F/4, 1,600 ISO

find themselves in. The 70mm, or wider end of things, is very useful for faces and small groups. It is just a bit longer than a 50mm normal lens. A touch of telephoto can go a long way.

Let's go back to the soccer game, shall we? You are hovering around the sidelines. Your kid has rounded up some teammates and wants a quick snap. A buddy portrait. Two, three or four kids, all goofing for your (roughly) 70mm lens. Perfect. Nice shot. Then they charge back onto the field for the second half. Slide that puppy to 200mm, and you've got a good working perspective on the action.

A handy lens, indeed. A 70–200mm telephoto can reach into the middle of a sports field and also across an Istanbul street into a spice market. At its long end, it can bring you in tight to the human face, rendering a beautiful, detailed portrait while minimizing background. In its wider settings, it is excellent for general scenes where storytelling is important.

The "go-to" 70-200 in my camera bag has a maximum aperture of f/2.8, which classifies it as a "fast" lens in photo lingo. As discussed in the aperture section, the lower the number, the wider the lens opening. In the world of telephoto lenses, fast and fixed are generally positive terms. "Fast" means the lens opens wide relative to its length; "fixed" means that the aperture doesn't change as you zoom in. In other words, if my lens is set at f/2.8, and I have to quickly zoom from 70mm to 200mm, the lens will stay at f/2.8. My exposure and my shutter speed will also stay put, right where I set them. (Unless the camera is set to P mode: Then it will make automatic adjustments. If set to A mode, my f-stop stays the same, but the shutter speed might adjust, depending on the scene.) I value that constancy. It's one less thing to worry about in the midst of all the other stuff out there waiting to jump me.

Fast and fixed aperture telephotos tend to be a bit expensive. There are now, however, a variety of telephotos on the market in the 70–200, 70–300mm ranges that are quite good and a bit cheaper; they are referred to as "variable f-stop zooms." A popular range of f-stops for these lenses is f/3.5 to f/4.5 or f/5.6. When you zoom a variable f-stop lens from wider to longer, the f-stop will change. The lens will get "slower."

Why is this important? As you zoom to telephoto, and the lens closes the aperture down, your shutter speed needs adjustment to maintain the same exposure. In manual mode, you have to be conscious of doing this yourself, but if you are in one of the autoexposure modes, the camera does it automatically. With the aperture closing down (letting in less light), the shutter speed requires more time to compensate for that loss of light. A slower shutter speed combined with a long lens can make for shaky, out-of-focus pictures.

So be careful! Remember what I said about choosing wisely: If your mission is to shoot kiddie soccer and the games occur mostly in daylight hours, a variable f-stop telephoto could suit you just fine. There's lots of light outdoors in the daytime, generally speaking. But if the games are at night or your student athlete is, say, a basketball player running around in poorly lit gymnasiums, you may want to consider the more expensive, fixed, fast glass.

A tremendously useful lens like a fixed and fast long glass is not a specialty item. A 70–200mm does a lot for you, and it is all-purpose. Because of its midrange lengths, it is neither too heavy nor too bulky for a typical camera bag. But, despite its applicability to so many situations, it will fall short (literally) if you are going after more exotic and elusive subjects, such as wildlife.

Depending on your quarry, this very rewarding but arduous (and sometimes frustrating) kind of photographic endeavor can require something beyond 70–200mm. There are 300s, 400s, 500s, 600s and more. These very large conglomerations of glass in a tube may be essential should you embark on that once-in-a-lifetime African safari or wilderness trip to Alaska with the intent of getting great lion or polar bear pictures. Gigantic lenses such as these are weighty and extremely challenging to hold by hand. Therefore, other things have to come along to provide stability, like monopods and tripods.

In short, this gets to be a lot of

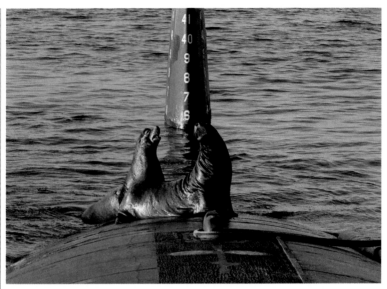

Sea lions on a submarine, 135MM, 1/125TH AT F/6.3, ISO 125

work. I advise venturing into these big-number lenses only if you are absolutely committed to a subject matter that demands their use. But yes: If, for example, birds are what make your heart take flight, then big lenses with a bunch of zeroes attached to both their millimeter lengths and their price tags are pretty much requirements. Beware as you enter this market. In the telephoto world, there are lenses (and companies that make them) that promise to do it all. One-stop shopping: "Yep, the Grand Master Zoomer! This here 65 to 892 millimeter variable f-stop son-of-a-gun with the hydraulically assisted autofocus and a built-in level is just the ticket! Leave your other glass home. This lens is all you need!"

Very seductive. And very untrue. Remember: The longer a lens zooms, the more distance those glass elements inside the barrel travel, with potential degradation of quality, sharpness, brightness and speed. At the camera store counter, play with the lens. Does if feel comfortable in your hands? Is the autofocus quick to respond? How heavy is the lens? Is it dark to look through? Is it a brand name? All of these factors affect how much use and enjoyment you will get out of your new lens in the field.

And, with lenses, the phrase "you get what you pay for" is very, very true.

MACRO SHOOTING

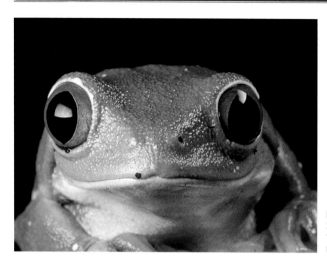

Frog closeup,
300MM,
1/200TH AT
F/40, ISO 100

I guess it can be called shooting. I mean, pictures are being made, right? But it's not in any way freewheeling, the way the term shooting implies. It's not chasing light or action or trying to capture that nuance of expression that defines a portrait subject.

● I have generally avoided closeup photo work. For me, this falls into the life's-too-short category. *Excruciatingly slow, tedious* and *painstaking* are all adjectives that come to mind.

But also, then: *beautiful, intricate, fascinating.*

Macro shooting is applied photography. It is not firing off frames for a lark. It is taking a camera and lens on a narrowly defined mission. There are parameters and concerns that make this exercise more of a study than "a shoot." Shooting small stuff can create big photographic headaches, to be sure, but venturing into the world of the very small can yield very large rewards.

Using a closeup, or macro, lens opens up an unseen universe to the photographer. From tiny flowers to minuscule bugs, there is much that is hidden, explosively colorful and dreamlike. Macros reveal texture and patterns that can be observed only as the camera moves relentlessly inward.

Concerns abound, as mentioned, many of them involving the issue of focus. Depth of field is razor thin

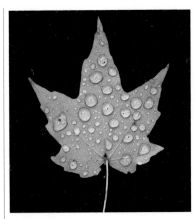

Leaf on asphalt,
105MM, 1/50TH AT F/10, ISO 200

when working close. Exactly how thin depends on the chosen f-stop and how near the lens is to the subject. Closing down the aperture to extremely small openings, such as f/22, f/32 and the like will increase depth, but it will also require longer and longer shutter speeds, which in turn mandate a tripod. No worries when the object is fixed, but for, say, a flower in a field, even the slightest of breezes will cause movement that a slow shutter speed will not stop. The result? A blurred flower.

A strategy for the above scenario is to go to "consecutive high" on the motor drive, or frame rate, of whatever camera you're using. Blasting through lots of pictures of a flower that does not change attitude or expression may seem excessive, but the fast-moving camera can, with luck, catch the posy just at that split second it is absolutely still. Sheer volume here can help accomplish the mission at hand. But then of course there is the issue of "mirror bounce." The interior workings of the camera as it swings the mirror up and out of the way of the sensor may in and of itself cause vibration at super-slow shutter speeds. Experienced still-life and closeup photographers often lock the mirror up after framing and focusing the shot.

Another way to increase depth of field without dangerously slow shutter speeds is to raise the ISO—and live with the resultant loss of quality. Yet another approach is to light whatever detail you're shooting with flash.

One thing I hope you are picking up on is the "horse trading" that goes on in almost every photographic strategy or equation. Want more depth of field? Okay, that means slower shutter speeds. Don't want that? Okay, jack up your ISO, and if you go really high ISO-wise, the picture will lose vibrancy. Want minimal depth of field for a portrait? Okay, but then part of the face might be a little soft, and the background will be completely out of focus, thus eliminating the sense of place. If that happens, you don't know where your subject is. No good, you say? I *need* to know where the subject is and what the environment is like. Okay, once again, close down your aperture, and lengthen your shutter speed. Oh, but a person might not be able to hold steady for that long a shutter. Well then, better use a flash. Or get a tripod. Or . . .

There are myriad minute calculations that need to be made as you approach any shot. As you shoot more and more frequently, these calculations will become not only more and more accurate, but also intuitive. One area where the calculations will forever be a bit more consuming and precise is in the world of closeup photography. The closer you are, the more unforgiving the tolerances that impose themselves.

With macro lenses and closeup techniques, it is a small world, after all, with smaller margins for error.

MOTION

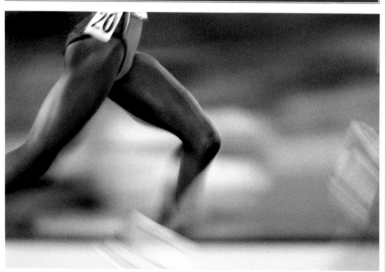

Panning with an Olympic runner, 600MM, 1/30TH AT F/4, ISO 400

We become desperate, on occasion, to stop the world. The great strength of photography is its ability to slice time and preserve moments. At many of the great news events of our era, there have been still cameras shooting side by side with video or motion film cameras. What do we, the general public, generally remember? The still image. My sense of history, and my memory, is written in still images. So how do you show motion when the camera in your hands is called a "still" camera?

● Hmmm . . . Another one of those photographic paradoxes. Remember when the aperture numbers got big, the opening got small? This is another one of those.

There certainly will come times when you'll want to show motion or, as I often put it, "the notion of motion" in a still frame. You'll want the viewer to know that this subject is on the go. Fast movement is a powerful thing to convey. It can signify importance (this person has to be somewhere in a hurry), a sense of emergency (even life-and-death situations) or effort and competition (runners charging, legs and arms pinwheeling into a frenetic blur).

Confronting a fast-paced world, we hold a camera designed to stop things dead in their tracks. What to do? Well, we can redirect the instrument, via the mechanism of shutter speed. As I've mentioned, shutter speed goes hand in hand with aperture. Together, they produce a proper exposure.

Remember when I said that each full f-stop click represented either twice or half the light, depending on which direction you were clicking? Same thing with shutter speeds. The speed of 1/250th of a second is twice as fast as 1/125th of a second, meaning it lets in half as much light as 1/125th. Go in the other direction, and the next full stop on the shutter speed dial is 1/60th of a second, which allows in twice as much light as 1/125th. It is a slower shutter speed than 1/125th.

(Please note that I am referring to the traditional full clicks on the dial, both for aperture and shutter speed. Most digital cameras now available have options in between the traditional full clicks of either the shutter speed or aperture dials. On the way to f/8 from f/5.6, for example, you can stop at f/6.3 or f/7.1. In between 1/125th and 1/250th live 1/160th and 1/200th of a second. These numbers may vary among camera systems.)

By adjusting your shutter speed, you can dictate whether you freeze a fast-moving object or let it blur through your frame to indicate motion. Obviously, faster shutter speeds stop things. Generally, it is accepted that to stop reasonably fast motion, your shutter must be no slower than 1/250th of a second. But, of course, there is fast—and there is fast. A basketball player at the top of his jump? A 1/250th setting will handle that pretty well. The overhand serving stroke of a top tennis player? No way. At 1/250th, most of the subject will appear sharp with a bit of trailing motion in the extremities, such as arms, hands, legs and feet, which almost always move faster than the core of the body.

Experiment! Your camera is likely to feature shutter speeds as fast as 1/4,000th or even 1/8,000th of a second. Click around the dial. See what works. Remember as a general rule of thumb: The closer the action is to you, the faster it will move through your frame, relative to your position.

PANNING AND BLURING

There is a difference between "panning" and "blurring." Blurring of your subjects may occur when you use a slow shutter speed (just what counts

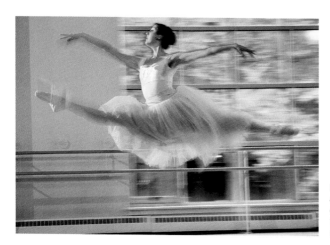

**Panning
a leaping
dancer,** 87MM,
1/125TH AT
F/6.3, ISO 200

as "slow" will vary relative to the speed of your subjects). Hold the camera steady, then let the subjects just flow through the frame, creating their own patterns and swirls. With blurring, a workable range of shutter speeds could vary from 1/15th to about 1/60th of a second. Obviously, a slower shutter produces greater blur, creating more of an impressionistic look for the subjects while, because you are holding the camera still, the world around them remains sharp and discernible.

Panning is different. Again, you need to choose a shutter speed that will produce the hint of motion for the subject. A ballerina at Lincoln Center will require a different set of shutter speeds than, say, a toddler at her dance recital. But the technique here, different from simple blurring, involves moving your camera and lens along with the subject. That way, the world

dissolves into a blur, and the subject, if you do it right, will stay approximately sharp. Panning takes practice! It can be a wonderful technique at a horse race, a car race or, as you see on page 67, a foot race.

Quick note: When I pan the camera with a moving subject, I don't generally like to use a tripod, even though there are shooters who would insist that it is essential for this technique. I find it gets in the way, actually impeding the fluidity of the movement I need to make as the action crosses my view. One good thing that happens as you slow your shutter in order to pan with action is that, correspondingly, your f-stop has to close down to maintain proper exposure. That means you pick up depth of field. The extra range of potential sharpness is very handy when everything, including the camera, is in motion.

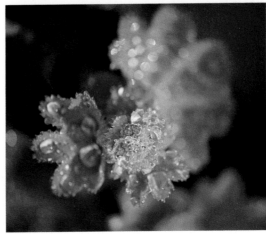

1) 1/800th at f/3.3

[SHALLOW DEPTH, DEEP DEPTH]

"Closing down the lens gains you back some of the depth you lost when you pushed in close."

● There is no better way to see depth of field disappear than to use a lens in close. The closer you get to your subject, the more and more minimal the depth of field.

Many of the new cameras, both pro and "prosumer," have lenses in their lines that will go to closeup, or macro mode. Some are all-purpose lenses that can be shifted for close work with the flip of a button or switch. Others are simply called macro lenses, and they will seamlessly focus from normal working distances to really, really up close and personal.

Again, one characteristic all of these lenses share is increasingly limited DOF the closer they get to the subject. One way to compensate, of course, is to click the f-stop to a larger number, which represents the smaller aperture openings. Many of these closeup lenses have smaller-than-normal aperture options and will close down to f/32, or even f/45.

Closing down the lens,

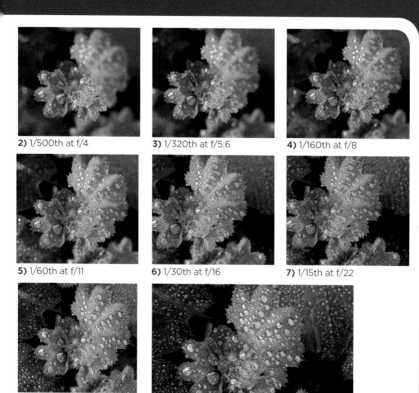

2) 1/500th at f/4

3) 1/320th at f/5.6

4) 1/160th at f/8

5) 1/60th at f/11

6) 1/30th at f/16

7) 1/15th at f/22

8) 1/6th at f/32

9) 1/6th at f/40

as already discussed, gains you back some of the depth you lost when you pushed in close. Take a look at this series of pictures, and watch, as they go from f/3.3 to f/40, the range of what is sharp increase in each sequential frame. Shallow depth of field to deep depth of field, with just a few clicks.

JOE'S TIP

For close-up shooting:

CHECKLIST:

❑ **Use a tripod. Shooting handheld closeups is tricky.**

❑ **This is an opportunity to use a cable release, which keeps your hands off the camera and eliminates any possibility of shake. I discussed this device and its use more fully on page 39.**

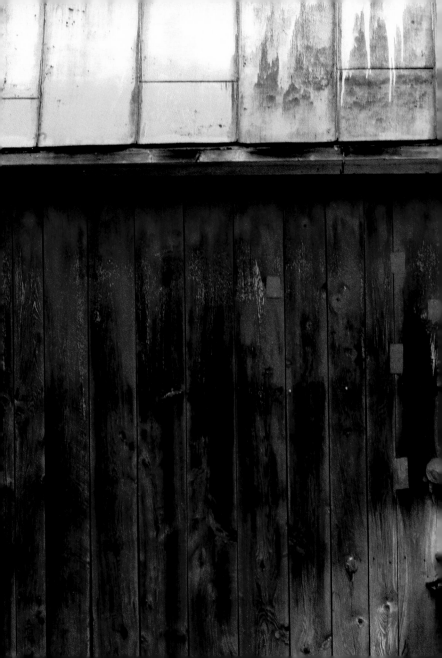

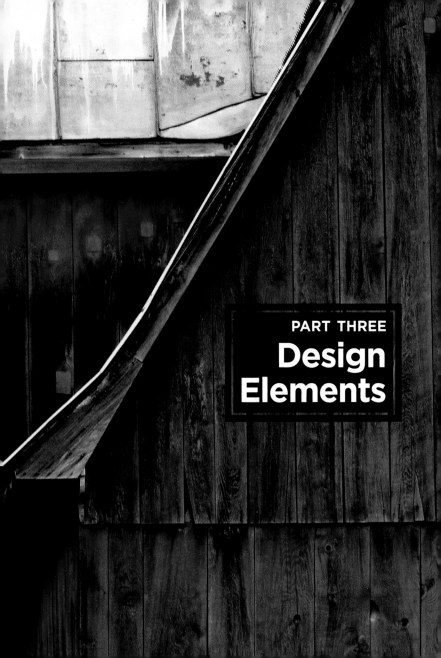

PART THREE

Design Elements

TEXTURE

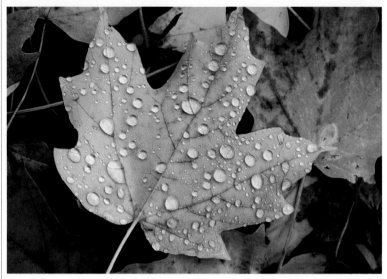

Drops of water on a blanket of autumn leaves, 105MM, 1/100TH AT F/10, ISO 200

Ever see a picture you could smell? Or one that made you itch, at least subconsciously? Chances are it is a picture filled with texture. Pictures that sum up phrases like "smooth as silk" or "hard as a rock" are generally studies of textures that both the natural and man-made world have to offer. When you hold your camera to your eye, remember to think about not only how a texture looks but also how it feels.

QUALITY OF LIGHT

The ever-important photographic constant, quality of light, has to be right there with you in an adventure with texture. Soft light drapes itself on silk, for instance, the same way silk drapes itself on our bodies. Hard sidelight thrown on sand, for example, creates the minute, endlessly repetitive shadow and light pattern that reminds us of how scratchy it is. This is very powerful because you engage not only the viewer's eyes but also the gut and the memory.

If you can make a person flinch with a picture of the shiny, metallic edge of a razor or shudder with cold at a picture of snow crystals, you're cooking. You've hit them not only between the eyes but also in the heart.

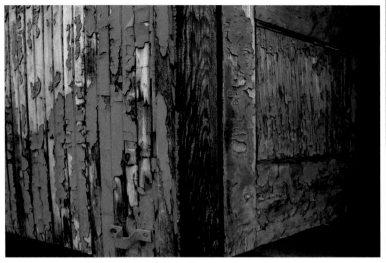

Peeling paint on a fence, 15MM, 1/60TH AT F/5.6, ISO 200

SENSORY AND TACTILE TEXTURE

Texture abounds. It is everywhere, in both the natural and manufactured worlds. Texture is a measure of how closely all of our senses are interconnected. Texture, which is about touch, constantly beckons the camera, which is about a visual sensation. When you combine the appearance and details of a surface with the right light, the resulting picture engages not just the viewer's eyes but also his or her nose, fingers, tongue.

You can wrap yourself up in a good picture rife with texture in the same way you wrap yourself in a soft blanket. There's virtually no end to the reactions you can produce. You can make somebody go "Yuck!" or make a viewer put the photo down, run to the fridge and grab a bucket of ice cream, then add cherries and chocolate sauce.

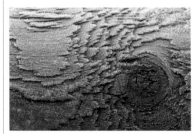

Coiled rope aboard a ship, 157MM, 1/10TH AT F/10, ISO 200

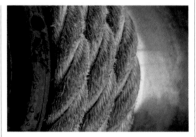

Grooves in the bark of a tree, 300MM, 1/6TH AT F/5.6, ISO 200

PATTERN

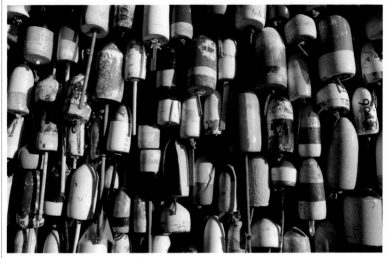

Lobster buoys, Cape Cod, 28MM, 1/640TH AT F/8, ISO 200

Observing patterns is one of the most arresting and intriguing things you can do with a camera. Patterns can be rhythmic and smooth, luring and lulling the eye as they roll out in endless fashion. Or they can be as sharp and loud as a drumbeat, stopping you cold with their jagged pace and color.

THE PATTERN GAME

As a photographer you play a game when your eye confronts a pattern: How much of it to show? How little? Do you embrace the entire pattern as the sole drama of the photo you are about to take, or do you truncate it, using the lens as a scalpel to slice only a piece of it? Yes, a pattern is interesting—but a pattern interrupted can prove even more interesting.

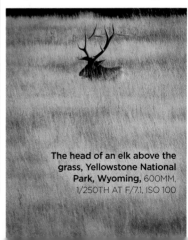

The head of an elk above the grass, Yellowstone National Park, Wyoming, 600MM, 1/250TH AT F/7.1, ISO 100

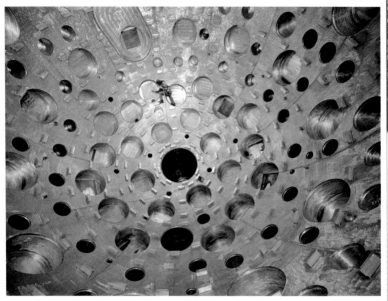

Test chamber in the National Ignition Facility, California, 24MM, 1/60TH AT F/5.6, ISO 100

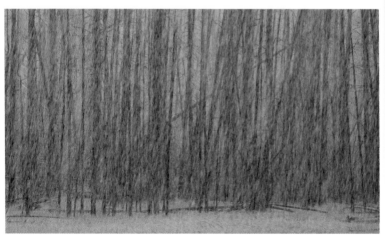

Rain in a forest of lodgepole pines at Yellowstone, 255MM, 1/20TH AT F/13, ISO 100

LIGHT AND FORM

Light is the variable here. Forms are forms. They will be the same tomorrow as they are today. But they will look different, depending on the light. As photographers, we follow light as surely as musicians in an orchestra follow the baton in the conductor's hand. Light hits things and defines them as being interesting or not.

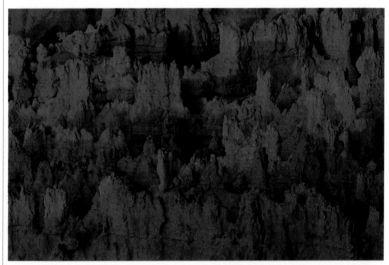

Bryce Canyon, Utah, just before sunrise, 180MM, 1/15TH AT F/11, ISO 100

LIGHT OBSCURES FORM

Hard light on surfaces, for example, illuminates those surfaces but causes other areas to go black. That play of light and shadow will draw the eye, which is programmed to seek light areas and is attracted by contrast. The edge of a highlight as it suddenly, sharply falls into shadow is a moment of high contrast that compels at least a glance. Don't be afraid of shadows! They are your friends.

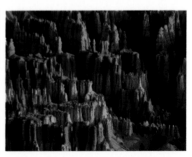

The sun highlighting rock formations at Bryce, 300MM, 1/10TH AT F/11, ISO 100

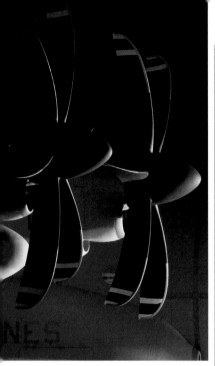

Hercules C-130J turboprop propellers,
450MM, 1/30TH AT F/10, ISO 125

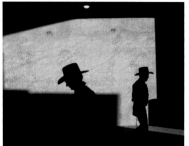

Silhouettes of cowboys, 85MM, 1/125TH AT
F/8, ISO 50

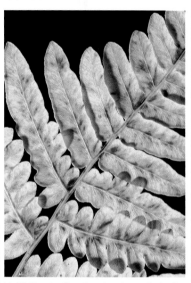

Light illuminating the structure of a leaf,
157MM, 1/60TH AT F/22, ISO 200

LIGHT REVEALS FORM

If shadow obscures form, soft light can reveal form in wondrous ways. While some forms call for that hard edge of darkness and bright light, others thrive in soft, diffuse illumination. Smooth, round shapes can often look best on a cloudy day. In this subdued light, details that would be hidden by hard, bitter daylight come forward and dominate. No shadow games here: The picture is filled with light, and the eye of the viewer is allowed to feast on nuance, detail, shapes and color. I don't want to talk about f-stops and ISOs here—we've already done that, and you understand the mechanics—I want you to look at the light. Drink it in. Decide what to do with it.

79

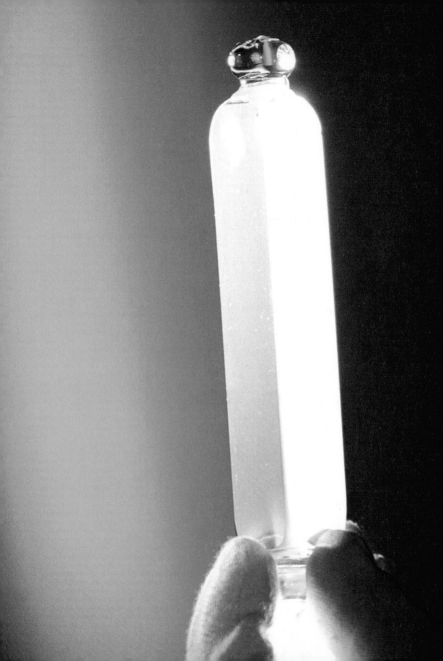

PART FOUR
Color

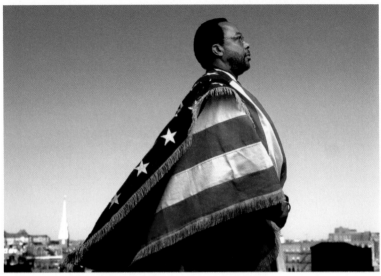

Red, white and blue of the American flag, 28MM, 1/1250TH AT F/8, ISO 100

We've talked about texture, pattern, light and form. There are pictures on these pages that show all of the above, from dead leaves to Baja bikers. What else was present in those photos? Color! You simply can't discuss pictures without talking about color, or lack thereof.

Take a trip back to—what was it?—fourth grade? Back when we first got acquainted with that notoriously colorful character, Roy G. Biv: red, orange, yellow, green, blue, indigo and violet. The colors of the rainbow. The color wheel. (There will be a test in tomorrow's class!)

THE COLOR WHEEL

There are folks out there who have spent their whole careers writing learned textbooks on color and how it interacts with our eyes. Do you need to do the same in order to pick up a digital camera? Blessedly, no. I mean, there's lots of color out there—an unfathomable amount of color. In our digital world, there are 16.7 million possible colors in an 8-bit image.

Sixteen point seven million. Has anybody seen them all?

No. But to get a handle on their vast variety, we generally organize colors using one of the two major

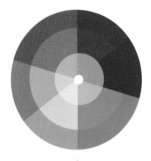

Warm | **Cool**

systems: additive and subtractive. Digital cameras and computers use the additive system with red, green and blue as the primary colors. Most printers and other methods of reproduction use the subtractive system with cyan, magenta and yellow (mixed with black) as the primary colors. The traditional subtractive color system, which painters and other visual artists (like photographers) have relied on for centuries, uses red, yellow and blue as the primary colors. Mixing together two of these colors produces the secondary colors:

• Blue + Red = Violet
• Red + Yellow = Orange
• Yellow + Blue = Green

Add these six to what are called the six "tertiary" colors (red-violet, blue-violet, blue-green, yellow-green, yellow-orange and red-orange) and you have the basic color wheel known to anyone who ever picked up a crayon.

Color relationships are easy to understand when illustrated on a wheel. The color wheel at left shows the six basic colors: the three primaries and the three secondaries. Colors that lie opposite each other on the wheel (blue and orange, red and green, yellow and violet) are known as "complements." Colors that lie adjacent to each other are called "analogous" colors. This wheel also depicts two other key attributes of color: hue and brightness. Hue is how you describe the color on the spectrum—in other words, "red" or "blue" or "yellow" or "green" or "violet" or "orange" (and on and on . . .). "Brightness" refers to a color's tone, whether it is light or dark. A third key attribute, saturation, refers to the intensity of the hue. A fully saturated hue is pure and undiluted. A desaturated hue moves toward gray, as if mixed with its complementary color (for example, red in shadow will appear greener). Note that one half of the wheel, from yellow to red, is marked "warm," and the other, from violet to green, is marked "cool." Colors have many attributes, including temperature.

As photographers, we seek to use the primary and secondary colors in strong, rich ways; they can be the tent poles that your picture hangs on. They have power. Why do you think pictures of the American flag grab your eye? Those saturated reds and blues command attention. You can use the same colors with more muted effect, too. Desaturated reds and blues can turn into dusty roses and slate blues that create an aura of melancholy or nostalgia.

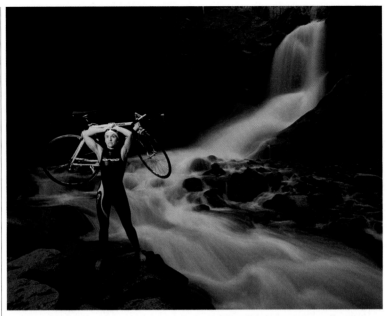

Calming blue water allows the subject to pop with a sliver of orangey yellow,
85MM, 2 SEC. AT F/4, ISO 100

TEMPERATURE AND SCHEMES

Take another look at the color wheel. Is it necessary to spin this wheel in your head while your eye is to the lens? Not really. Most of the time, your brain is either consciously or unconsciously aware of the color palette in the frame. One thing to remember is the notion of "cool" and "warm" colors. Take a look at the wheel yet again—note the zones of color temperature there. Using a monochromatic, or one-color, palette, can convey a particular mood, such as a swirl of red that screams, "Passion!" Cool green can evoke a rich—think "color of money"—vibe.

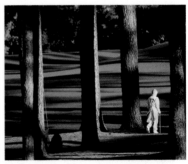

Golf course with cool greens, warm browns and a highlight of yellow,
600MM, 1/250TH AT F/4, ISO 100

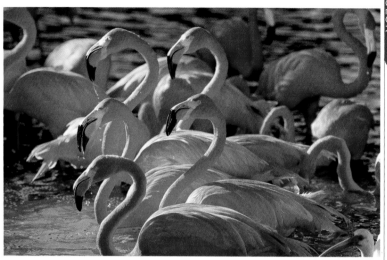

A blue-green pool provides a complementary background that enhances the warm pink-orange of the flamingos, 200MM, 1/1000TH AT F/4.8, ISO 200

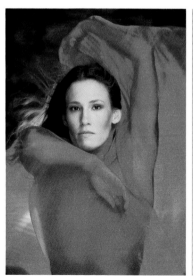

Red catches the eye and creates an intense mood, 190MM, 1/25TH AT F/5.6, ISO 400

Playing colors off one another can be very powerful. For example, focusing on the bright yellow overalls of a park employee as he strolls through the lush green grass of a golf course is making an analogous color scheme work for you. Or note, above, the deep blue-green water against which the vibrant pink-orange of a flock of flamingos comes alive, the cool color complementing the warmth of the birds' feathers. Complementary colors can work for you; hues opposite each other on the color wheel play well together, creating a vibration that attracts the human eye.

85

Breakfast in Copper Canyon, Mexico, 180MM, 1/30TH AT F/2.8, ISO 200

[POW! ZAP! WHAM!]

"Color, marching in lockstep with the advance and migration of light, moves. It's like the ocean. You don't want to turn your back on it for very long. Keep attuned to changes in color palette and in direction of light."

● I've got a strong color palette. Some folks in the photo world would be embarrassed to admit such a thing these days, when so much emphasis is placed on lack of color. There are a lot of looks popular today that are marked by desaturated colors—very hip, very cool. Very now.

I say, fine. Photography's a big room, and there's space for everybody. But as said, there are millions of colors out there, and me, I like 'em all. Color is so powerful when it is used well. It can beckon seductively or demand that somebody take notice. It can be as brutal as a bludgeon or as delicate as a scalpel. Color pours through our lenses and fills our eyes.

I went to five different grammar schools. And on top of that I had older sisters. Oftentimes I had to make my own fun. Early reading material ran to the comics, superheroes, epic adventures, tall tales and stirring battles. In other words, the fantasyland of my head.

Comic books contain stories told with vibrant, saturated color—smack-you-between-the-eyes, primary, slam-dunk color.

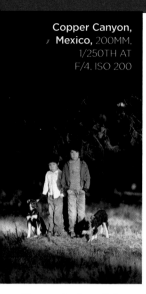

Copper Canyon, Mexico, 200MM, 1/250TH AT F/4, ISO 200

The panels of a well-done comic are their own color wheel, with vibrating colors, harmonic colors. For better or worse, strong colors have stayed with me.

That's not to say I'm out there shooting my own version of a comic book, though I have had some editors think this when I brought back my pictures. It's more about seeing in color and, over time, becoming aware of which colors play well together. It's also about being mindful of how powerful lack of color—or, certainly, selective color—can be.

Take a look at the early-morning scene in the Copper Canyon of Mexico, opposite. Members of

the Tarahumara Indian tribe still live a secluded life, deep in the canyon, as far removed from cities and tourists as possible. Simplicity of life, simplicity of scene, simplicity of color. The fog is like a gauze over the lens, draining hue and vibrancy—a perfect situation to shoot in color.

Really? Yes. Lack of color often makes as powerful a statement as a picture chockablock with reds, yellows and blues. Here, the pinprick of the orange fire in the midst of the pale morning brings home the feel of the start of the day. Early morning, cooking breakfast, hungry kid, dog running about—the same dawn-of-day ritual occurs in Chicago, albeit in a different way. That story is universal and very human.

Be careful, though. Color, marching in lockstep with the advance and migration of light, moves. Keep attuned to changes in color palette and direction of light. Early-morning (and late-afternoon) light is often called "golden hour" because the light is warm in tone and, as has been mentioned, angular, low to the horizon. Remember the color wheel? Golden hour lives in the warm section of the wheel.

DO THIS FIRST

Make the decision that the subject deserves color—and then decide what kind of color. There is color, and then there is *color*: There's the bright red of a fire truck at high noon and the soft greens of a still pond at daybreak. Color relates more to exposure than to most other adjustable elements. You can make color appear more lush or saturated by a subtle underexposure, and that image will have a different aesthetic and emotional power than one that might be bleached out or overexposed. With color, there's no right and no wrong, but there is *what you want*. So I urge you to develop a strategy. Do you want to further soften that pond or strongly brighten that truck? You can do this with your exposure setting before you click.

That morning in the canyon, the fog evaporated, opening the door for early, yellowish morning sun. Minutes after I saw that pale breakfast scene, I turned and saw the two boys, above left, awash in warm sunrise glow. It was like someone had peeled back

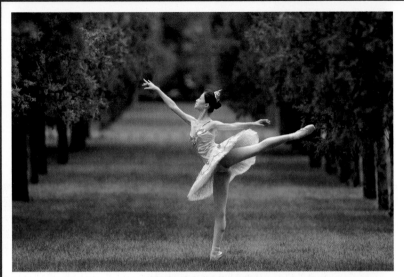

En pointe, 300MM, 1/350TH AT F/2, ISO 200

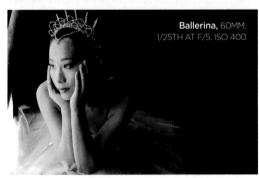

Ballerina, 60MM, 1/25TH AT F/5, ISO 400

a sheer curtain to unveil the true colors of the scene. Minutes apart, yet completely different color palettes. Stay on your toes!

Color is powerful because it commands attention. Color can represent the signposts you place in the wilds of your photograph. If you view color as part of the language of photography, imagine sparks of color to be exclamation points. They say, "Look here now!"

Instead of shouting and pointing, though, equally powerful statements can be made with muted, hushed color. Color that permeates but does not dominate. Color that creates a mood that is so pleasing or involving that the viewer surrenders to it. Soft color. Color without edges. Here is where clouds are your friends. When the sun is high in the sky, unrelenting and raw, color vacates. It surrenders, really. The strong sun blasts color, making it tinny and hard and rendering the shadows so black they are impenetrable. High noon, with its harsh daylight, is, as I've mentioned in the lighting section, the worst of times to shoot pictures, especially color pictures.

But lush color is a gift of cloudy weather. The clouds run between us and the sun, acting as a giant diffuser, and the light beneath the clouds falls as softly as a leaf. Here rich, saturated colors step forward and dominate. Take a look at the ballerina, opposite below, looking through a window on a cloudy day. The light embraces her face in a lovely fashion and slowly fades as it runs over her pink tutu. It gives the garment a richness that pleases the eye but doesn't overtake her lovely expression. It fits the quiet contemplation in the dancer's face.

Now bring a pink tutu outside into cloudy weather. As you can see, oposite above, it plays well with the complementary greenery. Neither color shouts, but each speaks strongly. There's a difference.

I've been discussing selective color, accents of color and quiet color. What about a color riot? That can be fun, too—in fact, unbelievable fun, if you can find the right scene or subject. LIFE assigned me to do just that—have fun with color—when they sent me across the

JOE'S TIP

We've talked about color theory and the color wheel—all well and good. But when you have a camera in your hands, how do you actually shoot color?

Remember the time of day and the atmospheric conditions will directly affect color. I have often said a perfect day for a shooter involves a stunning sunrise-sunset combo, with soft clouds in between those colorful bookends of the day.

The day I just described means that "golden hour"—that early and late time for light when it is warm, angled and beautiful—will be absolutely killer (worth getting up for!) but in between, there will be the soft light that comes through clouds and ensures rich, textured color, as well as easygoing, workable light for portraits. One thing the day described above has no room for is that screamingly hard quality of overhead, bright, high noon sun, generally the enemy of color and the photographer, out there on hot tarmac, trying to manage a few million overheated pixels. High, hard sunlight is generally to be avoided—bad light, bad shadows, bad results.

Now there might be shooters who will disagree with the above. Lord knows, photographers will disagree about anything. I have seen, and will continue to see, excellent pictures made at that time of day. And anyone who does take a camera in hand with serious intent will, despite his or her best efforts and intentions, occasionally be hooked into shooting pictures in that kind of light. Let me offer some survival strategies for finding good light and reasonable color in these conditions.

First, get out of the sun. Find open shade from a tree or a building. Most likely, you can manage that light. Look for reflected light. Glass and metal buildings can often make for huge "bounce cards" that reflect hard light in interesting or pleasing ways. In shade or reflected conditions, color often comes back to life, and you can see details in shadows. (Buildings painted white, obviously, are great "fill cards." Buildings painted different colors, or perhaps made of brick, will also reflect hard sun. But take note: Light bouncing off a structure painted, say, green, will cast, yes, green light on your subject. Which might be interesting-looking in the sense of being different, but it could also produce odd, sickly results. It is important to (continued on page 91)

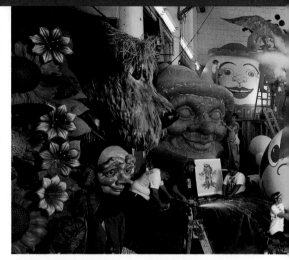

river from Manhattan to the Hoboken, New Jersey, warehouse where Macy's keeps all of its Thanksgiving Day floats. My job? Make a wide, wide picture, right, that showed the playful parade that rolls downtown from the Upper West Side to 34th Street every year on Turkey Day, delighting millions.

Fun doesn't even begin to say it. I was like a kid in a candy store, asking the mildly exasperated Macy's technicians for a smoking dragon, Humpty Dumpty, giant eggs, dwarves, flowers, reindeer, you name it—the kitchen sink of fantasyland. Each frame was just brimming over with color. Here, I was not really looking for that delicate color accent to entice my viewer's eye. I was opening the floodgates, filling the scene and the eyes with a full spin of the color wheel.

Out on the street, when it was time to go, the clown revved up the primary-color engine with this multihued smile. The brassy quality of light at eight in the morning, with no clouds to baffle the sun, was a perfect complement. Any later and the higher

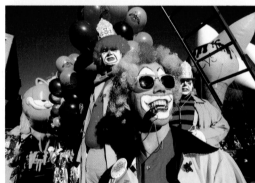

Macy's Thanksgiving Day Parade, 28MM, 1/125TH AT F/11, ISO 64

sun would have bleached these colors and cast my subject's eyes in deep shadow. I asked the clown to turn in the direction of the light, to work with it and not away from it. For snappy, contrasty color like this, the sun has to be with you, at your shoulder, and not ccbehind your subject.

The result is like an explosion in a paint store. Color splashing everywhere and over everything—celebratory, riotous, glorious color.

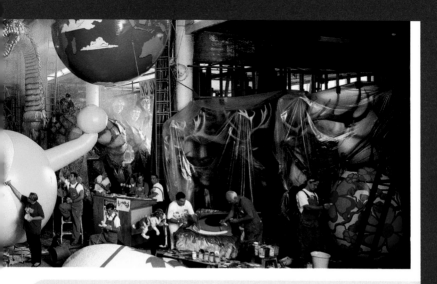

JOE'S TIP *(CONTINUED FROM PAGE 89)*

remember that light picks up the color of its reflector, so it may be best to seek neutral surfaces when looking for reflected light.)

Or just go inside. It's hot out anyway. Maybe that little coffee shop or that old bar down the street has a vintage wooden floor that will take nasty, unworkable sunlight and bounce it upward into the rest of the room to jam it with a golden glow. (Because light picks up the color of what it hits, old wood floors punt back warm, yellowish light, which is often very pleasing.) Buy a latte and sit by the window. The harsh light that was trashing everything in the street might meet a lace curtain or a set of blinds that shapes and bends it into something nifty-looking.

Remember, your fancy-pants digital camera has limits to what it can see. The eye, amazing instrument

that it is, can make minute, constant adjustments, and thus rotate from a bright, squinty-eyed street scene to looking into shade and pulling out detail. Even the best of digital cameras fail at this. So you have to give this tool an assist by being smart in these conditions. Move. Follow the light. That's where the color is.

CHECKLIST:

❑ Light reveals color, so follow the light.

❑ Golden hour is great light, but it often lasts less than an hour; it can be more like 10 minutes. When you see it, shoot it! Now!

❑ High, hard sun is tough but not impossible to shoot in. Look for bounce surfaces and diffusers, such as curtains, to help you.

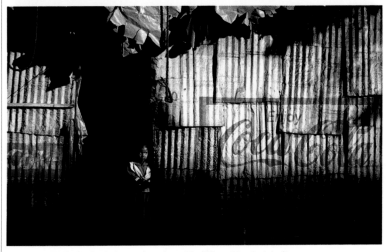

A young girl finds shade in an abandoned building, Mumbai, India,
180MM, 1/125TH AT F/4, ISO 100

I've already said that light is the language of photography. There are some who would say color is a second language, and indeed it is. So what are we talking about when we speak of photography's particular brand of colorful language?

THE LANGUAGE OF COLOR

Before breaking down the specific color components of light, let's get this on the table right away: The human eye is programmed—genetically, biologically, every which way from Sunday—to seek, be attracted to and thus look at light areas. The eye gets pulled by brightness. It's fact.

That is why it is so crucial to manage the tonalities of your picture. Don't expect someone to stay with that delicate little rose you found so attractive on your last photo walkabout if you place it against a big expanse of bright white sky. The viewer's eye will run right over that flower, hit that sky and keep going. It can't help it. If you carelessly include blown-out, dead-white areas in the edges of your frame, you are creating an exit ramp for someone to get out of your picture. And they aren't coming back.

That's the general rule of thumb for managing bright areas: Be careful! Small bits and pieces of extreme highlights are often fine. White, after all, is white. But if you need to put on sunglasses to look at your camera's LCD because a whole bunch of the pixels in there have died and gone to highlight heaven, you have a problem.

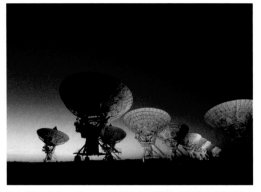

Satellite dishes at sunset, 20MM, 1/15TH AT F/5.6, ISO 100

COLOR ALCHEMY

When dealing with the specifics of color, it is good to remember three key attributes: hue, saturation and brightness. Hue is the color, plain and simple. Saturation deals with the intensity of that color. Desaturated colors are weaker, paler. Saturated colors are strong, powerful. Again, think of the American flag: It is a statement about saturated color. Brightness is about tone. If the tone runs toward darkness, it is called a "shade." If it leans toward white, it is a "tint."

These terms are nice to know and drop during the meet-up

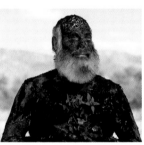

Dr. Andrew Weil in color, 105MM, 1/250TH AT F/5.6, ISO 100

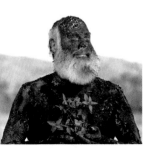

Dr. Andrew Weil in infrared, 105MM, 1/125TH AT F/5.6, ISO 100

of the local camera club, but by my lights they do little for you in the field. Color is a gut call. You feel it in your head and your heart. Colors have harmonies, vibrations. They call to your eye. Experiment with your camera and find out which colors, and combinations of colors, move you. Work on choosing the right hues, saturations and levels of brightness you need to tell your story, set your mood.

For an extreme example, look at the photos at left of alternative medicine guru Andrew Weil, naturally exposed in color and rendered in infrared. Both work, albeit quite differently. Which do you prefer? What are you after?

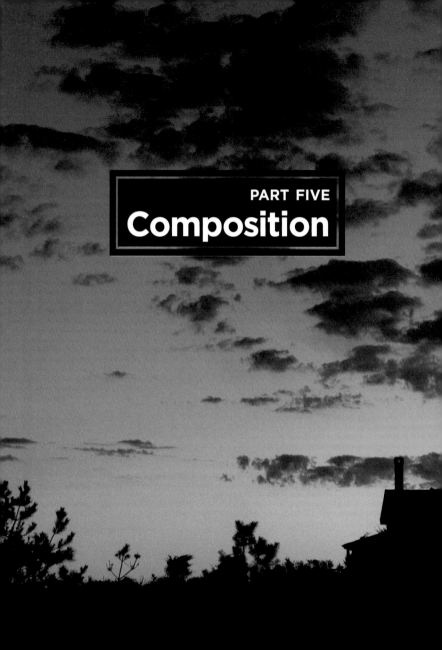

PART FIVE
Composition

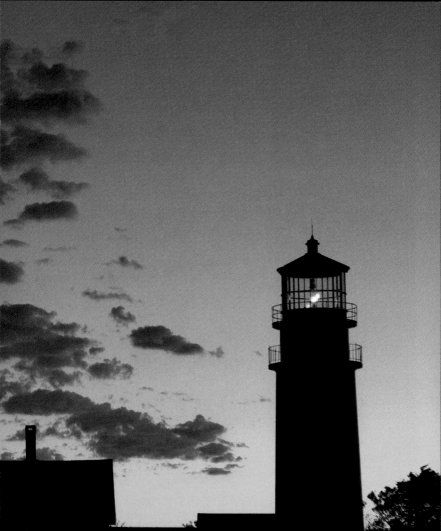

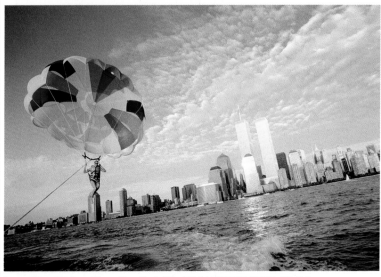

Parasailing, Hudson River, New York City, 35MM, 1/250TH AT F/11, ISO 100

"Composition" does not appear on a pull-down menu. It is not a checkoff. It's not a "maybe sometimes you might want to shoot in 'vivid' color mode if the light is flat" type of thing. It is with you all the time, every picture. Even for those of you who use a point-and-shoot or a cell phone and never ever resort to a setting, composition still pertains. There are tips to come for you, too, because any time you put the camera to your eye—in good light or bad light, at sunrise or sunset, framing people or landscapes—you are going to compose. Yes, you can crop post-click in Photoshop, but cropping is not delicate. It's a meat-cleaver technique; you're amputating part of your picture. It is better to see the picture whole when you are composing it.

THE FRAME

In my opinion, composition is everything. It first refers to what is in your frame and what is not. Composition derives from where you put the camera, and everything flows from where you put the camera. It is point of view. It is the best barometer of how you see the world and also what kinds of pictures you choose to make.

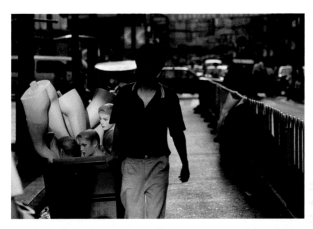

Man with a cart of mannequins, Shanghai, China, 200MM, 1/125TH AT F/2.8, ISO 200

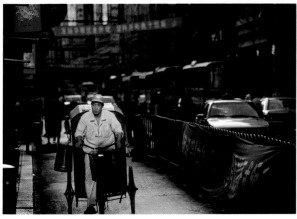

Man on a bike, Shanghai, China, 85MM, 1/125TH AT F/4, ISO 200

THE CONTACT SHEET

As I grew up in photography, I would routinely seek out editors, looking for work, asking for reactions, information, counsel, guidance. The top editors spent precious few minutes with your portfolio, your "greatest hits" if you will. They knew those snaps were your finest and had been edited, toned, tweaked, sequenced and printed to create impact and make an impression. That "best of" album could represent the salient images you shot in a day, or a week, or a year. They could be the product of an incisive, economical

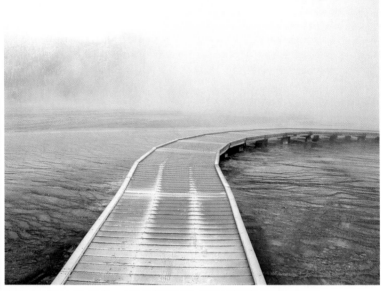

Walkway, Yosemite National Park, California, 27MM, 1/40TH AT F/8, ISO 100

mind at work behind the lens, a skillful storyteller who observed well. Or they could be the happy accidents of a scatter shooter who ran through jobs with finger continuously depressing "consecutive high" on the motor drive. The editors wanted to know which one you were.

To find that out, they went to your black-and-white contact sheets. These were the road maps to the way you saw as a photog: the telltale MRI of your photographic brain. These were all of your clicks. Did you zig when you should have zagged? Did you run out of steam at a certain juncture? Or did you see it through and construct a compelling document with a beginning, middle and end? Were most of your shots well composed? If you looked at my contact sheet from the street in Shanghai on the previous page, you'll see that the two pictures indicate that I varied how I used the light and my lenses. I kept moving and thinking. Take a look at your pictures from your last family outing. Is there variety of angles, lenses and light? Did you get in close for details and then move out to set the scene? Did you tell the story of the day? Think, constantly, about composition.

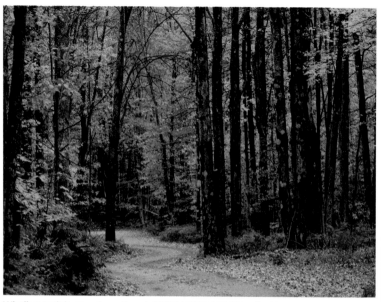

Winding path in an autumn forest, 200MM, 1/15TH AT F/11, ISO 400

THE NEW CONTACT SHEET
The contact sheet of today is the grid of thumbnail pictures on your computer. If you take a look at the results of any given foray into the field, you can deduce how you see, how you approach a picture or set of pictures. You can figure out what you want to do differently. You can even see your sense of composition evolve, right there on the screen. You can review your choices. Were they careless, haphazard? Or were they tight and to the point? Did you execute that mandate of good composition—in other words, take

responsibility for every pixel? Or did you just let something go, thinking: It will be okay?

Trust me, the editing process cannot put perfectly right a flaw that you bypass in your viewfinder, be it a small thing, like a tree branch coming out of someone's head, or a biggie, like a huge overexposed highlight patch at the edge of the frame. What you bypass in the field cannot necessarily be fixed on the computer.

POINT OF VIEW
Compose carefully! Look around the edges of the frame, not just in its

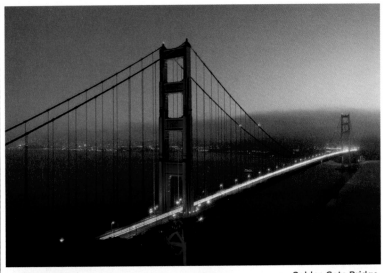

**Golden Gate Bridge,
San Francisco,**
31MM, 13 SEC. AT
F/22, ISO 200

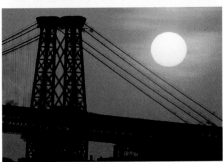

**Williamsburg Bridge,
New York City,**
400MM, 1/500TH AT
F/5.6, ISO 100

large center. Move your feet; consider an alternate view.

Once you have decided where the camera is pointed and what exactly is going to be inside that little rectangle we look through, then and only then should you start considering the smaller details in the frame—what stays, what goes, what's emphasized.

Camera position is the whole deal. Everything flows from that. Just like having a point of view in an argument, it needs to be incisive, logical, forceful—it's your opening statement.

RULES OF COMPOSITION

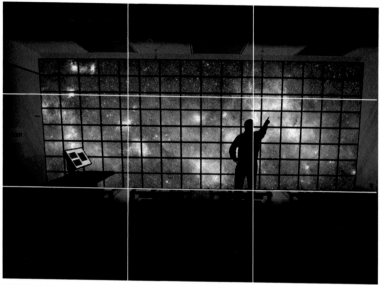

NASA's Advanced Supercomputing facility, California, 16MM, 1/20TH AT F/4, ISO 200

Yes, I did say earlier that "this is a game without rules," and that "rules are meant to be broken." But now we come to a section called "Rules of Composition." What gives? Well, with picture-making there remain a couple of tenets, or guidelines, that do make sense, over and over again. It's like getting eight hours of sleep at night: This is wise, solid advice. After eight hours, you generally function better than if you had broken all of the rules and pulled a Hangover night and woken up with a tiger in your bedroom and no knowledge of how it got there.

Similarly, if you obey certain rules of composition, you will generally be rewarded with better pictures.

THE RULE OF THIRDS

One of the most basic rules of composition is known as the Rule of Thirds. To employ the Rule of Thirds, imagine that two horizontal and two vertical lines divide your image into nine equal sections (as in the picture above). Then, place your points of interest along these lines. Basically, this rule means: Locate some of your points of interest outside of or on the barriers

101

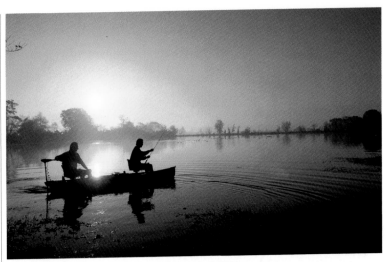

Silhouette of fishermen, 27MM, 1/640TH AT F/8, ISO 100

of that center box. There is nothing wrong with the absolute middle, but pictures are often more dynamic when the dominant focus is off-center.

Observe this rule, if not slavishly, then certainly on a regular basis. It goes back, way back, to before you and I were born. It helped Renaissance painters arrange landscapes and portraits, and it can help you arrange your photos. Look at the photograph above, for example, and then imagine the fishermen in the boat smack dab in the photo's center. The result is less than compelling, and points of interest are forced out of the frame. If I had framed the boat in the center, the image would have looked lifeless.

Because the whole intent of this book is to get you out of the gate, psyched about opening the shutter and creating memories that will last, some of the ancient aesthetic commandments—things that have worked forever for people trying to make nice pictures—need to be followed, or at least considered. Obey the Rule of Thirds, and you will be excited by the photographs you take. You will, no doubt, ask yourself all of the other questions photogs ask constantly: Which lens should I use? Should I move to the right? Can I ask them if I can take their picture or will they beat me up? Go long glass or wide? Why am I so unsure of myself? Why doesn't this get easier? *Why am I doing this?* But start with the Rule of Thirds when you look through the lens, and you're ahead of the game.

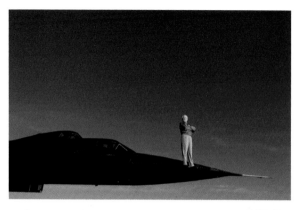

**Pilot on the
nose of a jet,**
24MM, 1/250TH
AT F/11, ISO 125

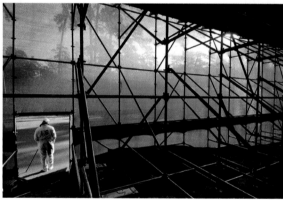

**Early morning
light at the Masters
Tournament,
Augusta National
Golf Club, Georgia,**
19MM, 150TH AT
F/8, ISO 100

It is such a powerful design formula that virtually every camera manufacturer offers a screen that you can drop into your viewfinder that divides that rectangle into thirds, both horizontally and vertically. I don't use them myself, preferring a blank slate (it fits my brain!). For me, being a bit of a traditionally trained journalist, the Rule of Thirds is pretty intuitive. Still, I like to pause every now and again to think about this rule, noting how well it usually works. Splitting sky and land on a 50-50 basis, for instance, often results in a static composition. Squeeze one or the other up and down into 1/3:2/3 ratio and feel your scene take on graphic punch.

Play with the thirds of the frame, up and down, left and right. You'll see your images change dramatically. You'll see them come to life.

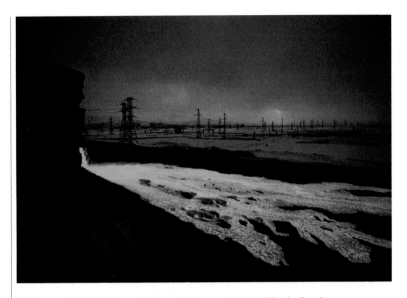

Molten metal flowing from rail cars onto frozen tundra in Siberia, Russia,
20MM, 1/30TH AT F/4, ISO 200

DISTILL

Less is often more. When you place lots of elements into a composition, it can start to look like a patchwork quilt. Generally, you don't want your viewers to be playing *Where's Waldo?* Where should I look? What's the subject? The busier a frame is, the harder it can be to decipher. Even the effective Rule of Thirds won't help you situate everything.

Remember that you will not necessarily be there to narrate your pictures. You can't sit with everyone who examines your images and whisper over his or her shoulder, pointing out the area of the frame that you found interesting. "See that right there? The guy with the funny hat? Isn't he great?" Your pictures have to speak for themselves; after you create them, their lives are their own.

FOREGROUND, MIDDLE GROUND AND BACKGROUND

For a picture to be effective compositionally, it has to offer a powerful, wordless road map to the viewer. It has to be readily apparent, through framing, light, color and arrangement of elements that someone is supposed to look right here, right now.

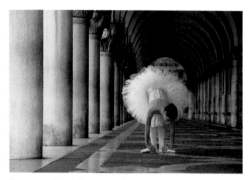

Dancer, 130MM, 1/40TH AT F/7.1, ISO 200

front of your lens, but if you don't anchor your foreground with something of true interest, nobody's going to look. Take the picture below, of Anna Canning, a young blind girl on a raspberry-picking expedition, as an example.

Here, the large green leaves jutting into the foreground work with the smaller leaves of the background to embrace Anna in a verdant shelter. Golden light fills the middle ground to draw our eyes to her intent expression as she feels for the berries. All three areas work to engage us.

To that end, remember that there are not only areas of the photograph left-to-right and top-to-bottom but also three-dimensional regions in a photo: foreground, middle ground and background. Once again, you are responsible for all of them, and they all have to work in concert. A busy or blown-out background can kill an otherwise worthwhile foreground.

You can have the prettiest, sweetest scene in the world in

Good composition is the hook that impels viewers to sign on to your photographic adventure. You go out into the world and have these very normal moments—or frenetic and altogether magnificent adventures—and you duly record them in pictures. That set of pictures, being viewed by Uncle Joe or another Joe who wasn't in the rain forest with you, has to be strong enough to bring the birthday party or the Amazon River right to the living room. If you have framed these pictures correctly, you can make your viewer feel just as you did when you were making them.

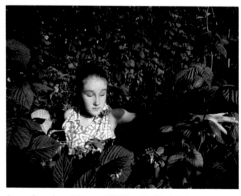

Anna Canning, 20mm, 1/125TH AT F/11, ISO 64

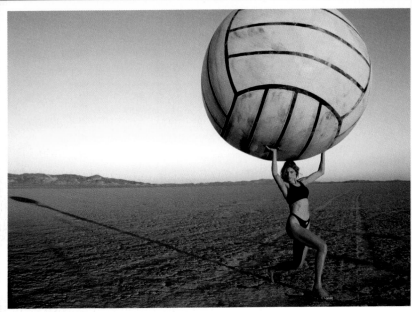

Gabrielle Reece, 28MM, 1/30TH AT F/11, ISO 100

[THIRDS, WORKING TWO WAYS]

● When dividing your frame into thirds, it is important to remember that the Rule of Thirds works both horizontally and vertically. Our eyes are arrayed in our head horizontally, so it is more natural to be conscious of arranging things interestingly in panorama, or landscape mode, because that is generally the way we see. It is easy to forget that the rule is just as valid up and down as it is across.

When LIFE asked me to shoot a story on a strong woman, pro volleyballer Gabrielle Reece was an immediate choice. She was Superwoman, beautiful and athletic. I posed her as Atlas, substituting a gigantic inflatable volleyball for Earth. In the horizontal shot above, there is hard, late daylight coming from camera right, hitting her and the giant ball, and throwing a long, dynamic shadow across the desert floor. Placing her in the extreme right-hand third of the frame allows the shadow to play out and the coolness of the deep blue sky to vibrate and interact with the warm tones of the cracked orange earth of the dry lake bed. There are lots of things here for the viewer to absorb—color vibration,

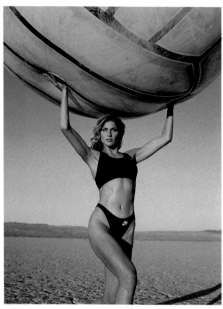

"When dividing your frame into thirds, it is important to remember that the rule works both horizontally and vertically."

Gabrielle Reece, 105MM, 1/125TH AT F/11, ISO 100

shadow games and compositional tension. They all derive from the camera's point of view and observing the Rule of Thirds horizontally.

I applied the rule in the vertical shot above, too. Gabby encounters the camera here in straightforward fashion, again heroically posed, holding up the volleyball-as-world. My camera angle is low, a useful tactic to use when working with athletes because when you look up at them, they will appear bigger than life. The desert is just a tone, striping across the bottom third of the frame, locating her. She gazes at the camera from the middle third, a simple blue sky framing her but not competing for attention. The top third is her burden, the curve of the volleyball.

Rule of Thirds. Remember that it slices both ways.

DO THIS FIRST

Test the waters, compositionally. Move the camera around, and move your principal subject left and right, up and down. Stay away from the common fault of putting your camera to your eye, your subject in the middle and going *click*. In other words, be as dynamic with the camera as you want your picture to be.

[SHOOT IT LOOSE! ROCK AND ROLL!]

"There have been times I have wanted to change the name of my location lighting workshops to 'Just Take the Picture Already!'"

DO THIS FIRST

When you want to enjoy a bit of spontaneous, rapid-fire shooting, prepare your camera for the task at hand. Set it on autofocus and take what I would call a "quickie Polaroid" of your setting, which will allow you to dial in the right exposure. Now put any concern about f-stops out of your mind, and fire away. This is an exercise in composition, not lighting, so think only about what you want in the frame. Later, analyze the results from that perspective: What's working compositionally—and what's not.

● Composition rules, as I have mentioned. But rigidity doesn't. Although it is important to govern your frame well, do so benevolently, not with an iron fist. There are pictures out there you just might miss while you are setting up a shot and putting your lines in a row along with your ducks.

I certainly can be careless at times; every photog will be, eventually. There isn't a shooter out there who hasn't either grimaced or flat out shouted at the computer screen when seeing an unpleasant, jarring something-or-other pop up when he or she just didn't see when the camera was to the eye. It is frustrating; when it happens to me, it prompts me to be really, really careful next time out.

There's nothing wrong with being careful, but there can be a lot wrong with being so meticulous that the world spins

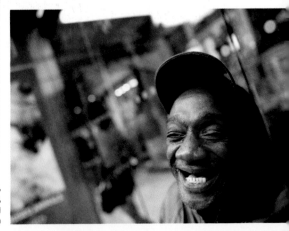

Having a laugh,
New York City,
28MM, 1/400TH
AT F/2.2, ISO 400

away in front of you while you carefully adjust your tripod. I teach a fair amount, and I have coached shooters on a location foray, then sat back and waited and waited and waited for them to release their shutters. Lots of minute adjustments or waiting for a subject to move her pinky just so. At times like this, I have wanted to change the name of my location lighting workshops to "Just Take the *Picture* Already!"

So, although it is advisable to be careful, composing well and exerting patience behind the lens, it can be equally important to just let it rip. Today's cameras are such finely tuned machines that they can usually expose and focus on their own. So take advantage, at least occasionally, of those systems. Get in the zone, know your exposure, let autofocus mode out for a healthy romp and just start shooting. I shot the picture opposite without the camera to my eye. This gentleman and I were having a lively conversation, and I was just about to push on (I had actually lowered my camera), when he simply cracked up laughing. I knew my focus sensitivity

would grab his face and that my lens was wide enough to establish the scene, so I just hit the shutter, set on consecutive high. I got several frames showing his amusement, and this one is just cockeyed and off-kilter enough to reflect his exuberance.

You can do the same thing anywhere. An excellent exercise for building your compositional muscles is to wander the streets and shoot pictures as you move through the crowds, without ever

putting your camera to your eye. Keep moving, and keep shooting. Shoot a lot. Shoot all day like this. Then take a look at what you've captured. You may be surprised to find that all that carefree clicking has yielded an energetic frame or two—or 20. The successful shots might be a touch out of focus and might not conform to the classic rules of composition. But an out-of-control adventure like this can liberate you. Go for it. Take your camera, and don't put it to your eye.

JOE'S TIP

Sometimes when you pick up your camera, your aim is to carefully render a subject. Sometimes it's to capture a special moment. Sometimes it's to create something artsy. And sometimes it's just to have fun—a bit of a photographic lark. That's what we're talking about here, so adopt a loosey-goosey mindset and a freewheeling plan to match. Having said that, make sure before you wade into any session of spontaneous shooting that you've got the right equipment and realistic expectations.

CHECKLIST:

❏ If the camera is to your eye, do try to establish the crucial spot of critical focus on your subject's near eye.

❏ If you're shooting from the hip, burst the camera: Get off a single frame, then go to consecutive high. You will produce some out-of-focus frames as you move, but you'll likely get some sharp, sweet frames, too.

❏ Whether you shoot from the hip or with camera to your eye, use a relatively wide lens. You want to capture a scene, you want to bring things in, and it's virtually impossible to do this kind of broad, fast shooting with a telephoto.

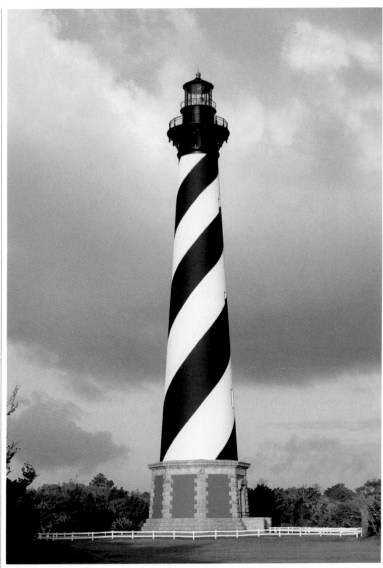

Cape Hatteras Lighthouse, North Carolina, 70MM, 1/2,000TH AT F/7.1, ISO 400

PICTURES WITHIN PICTURES

Indeed, as this section title says, there are often pictures within pictures. If you are in a place that you most likely will not be able to get back to easily, it is best to think aggressively and broadly, and not just content yourself with the "Oh, honey that's nice" roadside snap. If you can, get closer. Shoot that roadside pic, and then look for other things. Remember, the "big picture" is just the start of things.

PEELING THE ONION

Lighthouses are obviously fascinating visuals and, given their distinctive architecture, are highly graphic subjects to shoot. Moreover, these beacons are usually located in pictorially intriguing places. They have great allure for a photographer; I'd love to have a nickel for every picture that's been taken of a lighthouse.

But for me, a people shooter, dealing with buildings, no matter how historical or pretty, can get boring, and quickly. Yet, when confronted with this barbershop pole of a lighthouse in North Carolina, I got excited: I had good light, a graphically strong subject and freedom to move my camera about. I promptly determined to come away with something

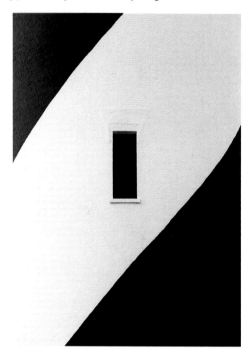

Closeup of Cape Hatteras Lighthouse, 155MM, 1/250TH AT F/8, ISO 200

that didn't look like the postcards they were selling at the gas station down the street.

First, however, I went ahead and shot the postcard. Done deal. This is advisable; pick the low-hanging fruit. Frame vertically, give the tower room to breathe at the top of the frame and arrange those wonderful clouds well. This is about patience and care behind

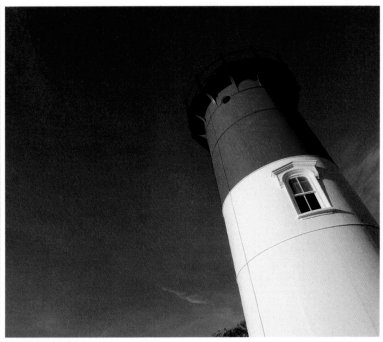

Wide-angle view of Nauset Light, Massachusetts, 21MM, 1/200TH AT F/13, ISO 100

the lens. At this time of the day, the light is good, and, if it hangs around and doesn't disappear completely behind low clouds, it will only get better. You've got an active sky, so shoot—and wait. Shoot—and wait. The clouds will move, the sunlight will get richer and warmer. Be careful of your lines. To my knowledge, there is only one well-known leaning tower in the world, and it is in Italy, and it is not a lighthouse.

Shoot, and shoot some more. Think of this: How long did it take you to get to the lighthouse? How many hours did you drive? You parked the car and unloaded your gear from the trunk and maybe even set up a tripod. That's a lot of work for only 5 or 10 frames, so stick with it. Watch the light and the clouds change. The building doesn't budge an inch, but the changing atmosphere will allow it to express itself differently.

After you've covered the basics, go for something different. This is a game professional photogs have played forever. We shoot what is needed—we shoot "the assignment," the shot

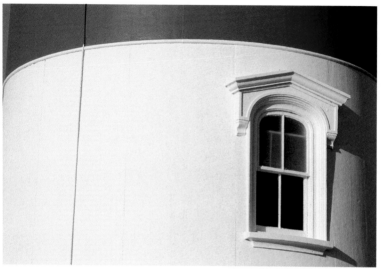

Nauset Light, Massachusetts, 202MM, 1/320TH AT F/13, ISO 100

of record, the shot that proves we got there—and then we dive in and experiment.

Try a very long lens, if you have one. Or focus in close to the structure with something very wide and play with distortion. Think to yourself: About a million billion photos have already been taken of this thing. How can mine be different?

An exercise such as this will make you a better photographer. On Cape Hatteras, I shifted to a long lens and wandered around the lighthouse, eventually finding the small, compositional exclamation point of the black window in the middle of the white sweep of the paint job. For the shot, shown on page 111, I bull's-eyed

the window, and let the building do the rest of the graphic work for me. There's no context here; I distilled the structure down to simple, pleasing blacks and whites. I already had the shot that shows it's a lighthouse. This one is about the character of the place, its uniqueness. (I really feel good about this frame. This view has been taken, I'm sure, only a couple hundred thousand times, not a million billion.)

Think of photo subjects as onions. You have to peel away layers. Shoot the outside, to be sure, then move in and peel back layer after layer. The picture that really rings true might just be living inside the picture you are already taking.

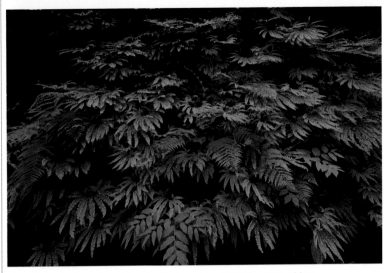

The clusters of ferns form triangles that create a dynamic composition,
19MM, 0.4 SEC. AT F/11, ISO 400

When you talk about composition, you have to deal a bit with geometry. Thankfully, not too much, because I stink at math. But the viewfinder frame we look through is, after all, a rectangle. And the shapes we fill it with—intuitively, unconsciously or deliberately—are often geometric.

COMPOSE DYNAMICALLY

Take triangles. They pop up quite frequently in effective photographic composition. The shapes of rooms and of certain elements of nature or landscape often form triangles. Or diagonals. Or leading lines.

Or converging lines. These are all geometric elements that draw the eye, lead the eye or create dynamic tension within that basic viewing rectangle. It is how we arrange these points of graphic tension that will determine whether we succeed in our composition, and therefore involve and excite our viewers, or whether we bore them. Paul Simon once said there must be 50 ways to leave your lover. I don't know how many ways there are to make someone leave a photograph, but dull, flat composition is a surefire one.

As a photographer, what you want to capture, besides the picture itself,

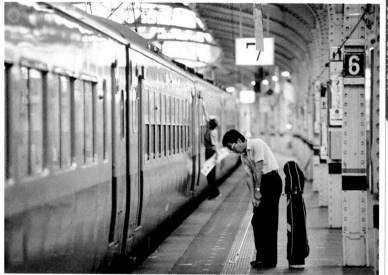

The receding triangles formed by the train and platform, flanked by the upright rectangles of the pillars, spotlight the golfer, 28MM, 1/250TH AT F/2.8, ISO 100

is the attention of the viewer—your consumer. Whether it's an editor or Aunt Edith, you want to make the person look and then stay with you. Accept this, please: The world is awash in visuals. Magazines sit on racks by the hundreds, screaming for attention. Everybody's blogging, hoping someone will notice. News channels drone on 24-7. All of your friends want to show you their vacation pix. People are subjected every day to a veritable fire hose spewing visual information. And here you come along with your picture, asking them to spend some time with it. Good luck.

That luck improves if you compose dynamically. If you don't nail it on the graphics in a heartbeat, your picture is

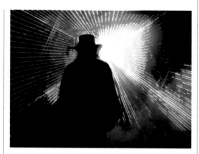

Strong lines of laser light draw the viewers' eyes to a performer's silhouette, 28MM, 1/125TH AT F/5.6, ISO 200

just a bunch of also-ran pixels as your viewer turns back to the latest news about Brangelina. Think of composition as the first impression you make on a first date. That impression had better

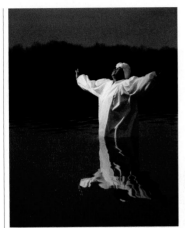

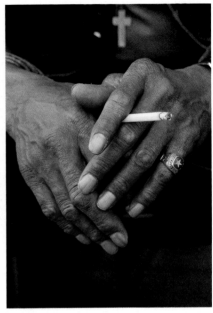

The minister's cruciform shape is repeated in her watery reflection, 85MM, 1/60TH AT F8, ISO 100

A football player's hands form an upside-down triangle, 200MM, 1/25TH AT F/11, ISO 400

be a good one, or that first date is also a last one.

Play with angles and shapes. Isolate them, group them or make them lead the viewers where you want them to go. Use diagonal lines to break up that staid rectangle you are looking through. On these pages and the previous two are some examples.

The green gaggle of ferns, on page 114, is really a collection of triangles, arrayed so that they fill the frame with engaging, repetitive shapes.

The line of the train and the platform, on page 115, brings you right to the subject, the golfer, practicing his game on the platform.

At a rock concert, also on page 115, the hot core of laser beams pulls you into the middle of the photograph, as the star leaves the stage.

A former football player's hands at rest, above, make their own upside-down triangle. You get drawn to the shape and then get involved in the weathered hands, which tell a poignant story.

The minister at left above stands in a river with her face and hands lifted toward the sky. Her arms and body form a cross shape that's mirrored in the water. Imagine this photo if her hands were at her sides. It simply wouldn't be such a powerful, evocative pose.

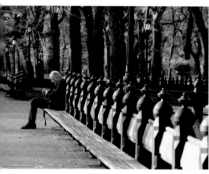

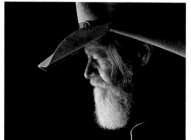

◀ **A row of park benches forms a line to the horizon,** 210MM, 1/160TH AT F/10, ISO 200

The cowboy's hat creates another triangle, 89MM, 1/120TH AT F/5.3, ISO 200

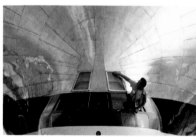

The glowing metal arcs of a NASA Guppy transport plane draw the eye to the worker's activity, 400MM, 1/250TH AT F8, ISO 100

Above right, the angled brim of the cowboy hat makes its own triangular top. Those lines direct the eye, and the upside-down V helps keep you in the frame and involved in the rugged face.

In the photo at top, an imposingly long stretch of park benches forms a riveting line that recedes into the far distance. The eye follows that line and encounters the lone graphic punctuation point: the early-morning visitor. Take him away, and the picture's impact disappears—it becomes just a bunch of empty lines. But now the lines lead to that man, and we share his bench with him.

In the photo above, the nose of this Guppy, a strangely shaped transport plane used by NASA, combines gleaming arcs and triangles. The sunrise shape pulls you straight to the featured activity: the early-morning cleaning.

Photographs, at the end of the day, just sit there, either on a screen or on paper. They don't sing and dance. They don't run and jump. It is an ongoing conundrum we always face as shooters: We hold in our hands a "still" camera, a machine designed to stop time and motion. So how do we make something static appear active and dynamic?

Good composition.

It can make a still photograph move.

PORTRAITS

To me, everything is a portrait. To quote friend and mentor Jay Maisel, "Everything has gesture." A person, a face, a rock, a tree—depending on how you shoot it, the subject expresses itself beautifully or not at all.

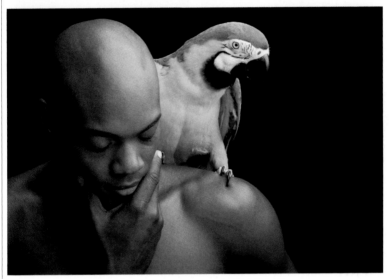

Portrait showing contemplation, 200MM, 1/250TH AT F/22, ISO 200

GESTURE AND EXPRESSION

Life moves; we have to move with it. The human face is ongoing theater, filled with nuance, subtlety and emotion. Beauty abounds. We have to find it. I've had glamorous models in front of my lens who have turned out to be brittle and boring subjects. And I've met folks on the street who, without looking in any way extraordinary, captivated me—I simply could not stop taking pictures of them.

To be a good portrait photog, even of your kid or best friend, you need a camera, a relentless curiosity and a hungry eye, always roving and looking. Other paramount requirements include a sincere empathy for the human condition, a well-developed sense of humor and irony, an understanding of human foible and ego, the ability to strike up even the most cursory of relationships with relative ease and the desire to tell stories. A pretty

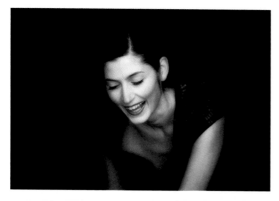

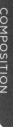

Portrait showing joy, 200MM, 1/200 AT F/8, ISO 200

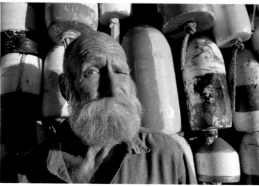

Portrait showing experience, 28MM, 1/400TH AT F/11, ISO 200

tough exterior, one that can handle rejection, helps—not to mention a level of confidence that pumps up and involves your subjects, making them, busy as they may be, willing to give you the time of day. You can say to your kid after her basketball game, "Give me a smile," and her answer might be, "No way, Mom!" You need to deal with that just as if the President of the U.S. of A. had said, politely, "Not just now."

You need passion. I swear some people, including my daughters, have given me time to work just because they sensed the urgency in my voice. I was able, somehow, to convey to them that this photo was important, that I needed to shoot it and that if they allowed it, I would do so well with it that the photo would become important to them, too.

The hard part is crossing the bridge, getting inside someone's natural barriers, making eye contact and gaining someone's permission without a word being exchanged, sensing body language and knowing when it's okay to approach and when it's time to back off. The sensitivity to know and respect boundaries is part of this, as is the grit to push beyond them when invited in.

You never want to push your subject around or trample his or her feelings or defenses. But you do want to get the true picture. It's not only professional photographers who find themselves in uneasy situations. An example: You're shooting your local high school football team on a regular basis. You know the players and the coach. Now it's playoff time. The quarterback throws a touchdown, and you are shooting the smiles and the jubilation. Then, in the last minute, he throws an interception, which causes the team to lose. You are in the locker room, faced now, not with whoops and shouts of joy, but with dejection, maybe even tears. Do you leave? Do you back off? Or do you risk disapproval, maybe even a confrontation, by lifting your camera to your eye and continuing to record the story of that game? Are you here as a friend or a chronicler? Do you suck it up and shoot, or do you fade away into the night, knowing that what you captured was incomplete? Or do you find admittedly conflicted middle ground and work quietly, from a respectful distance?

All these questions! It's complicated being a photographer.

TAKE A PIECE OF THE ACTION

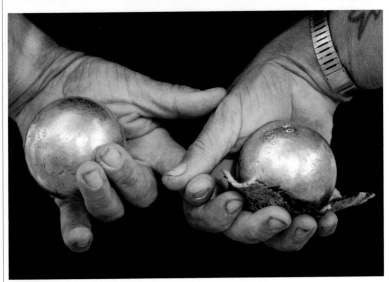

Hands of boules player between throws, 180MM, 1/250TH AT F/5, ISO 200

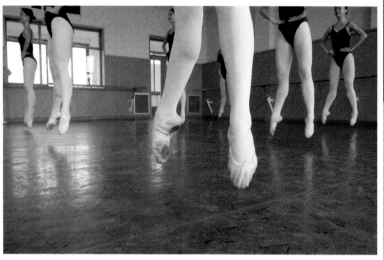

Dancers training at the Beijing Dance Academy, 27MM, 1/250TH AT F/4, ISO 400

A portrait can be defined in many ways. You don't necessarily need to see the subject from top to bottom to be moved, riveted or intrigued by who he or she might be. In fact, showing just a little can pique your viewer's interest and curiosity. It can also convey character.

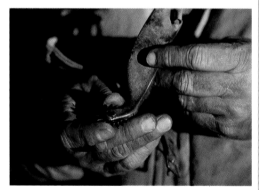

Hands holding stirrups, 200 MM, 1/125TH AT F/5.6, ISO 200

● I have always been a big fan of photographing hands. Hands can often tell the story of a life. What someone does helps to define who he is, as we've said, and what he does, he often does with his hands. Hands show the stresses, scars and grit of life. Think of hands on a baseball bat or the bow and neck of a violin.

Of course, if you are photographing a class of ballerinas, you may want to shift to the feet.

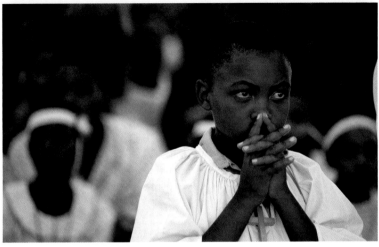

Boy praying, 200MM, 1/60TH AT F/2.8, ISO 100

When I am working with subjects, trying to make a portrait, I stay alert. People will do the darnedest, most natural, effortless, compelling things, and you have to be prepared for it.

● I keep my eyes on my subjects, even when one of them takes a cell phone call, or when we are just in between pictures. When they are not conscious of being photographed, they can simply revert to being themselves, and their gestures and body language become entirely natural. I have just about thrown myself at people when they behave like that, blurting, "Don't move! Please don't move!" Because in that off moment, they became a photograph.

Famous, true photo story: Ernst Haas, a wonderfully sublime photographer, was sent to photograph Albert Einstein. Haas's editor commanded him to "get a picture of Einstein thinking." Evidently Mr. Einstein was not cooperating, being very aware of the presence of a man with a camera. So Ernst asked him, quite innocently, where he had put a certain book. Einstein paused, and his fingers went to his chin in pensive fashion. His face said, "Now where did I put that book?" Ernst was ready, and he captured a photograph of Einstein thinking.

So keep your eye on your subjects. Be ready with a camera. The right gesture—the perfect moment—is fleeting. You see it, then you don't.

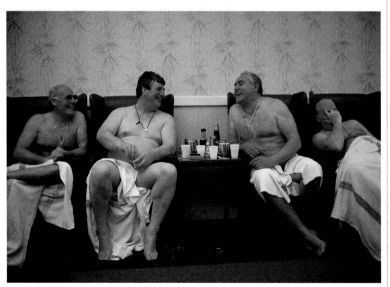

New York City firefighters on a lunch break, 105MM, 1/160TH AT F/11, ISO 400

Men in a steam bath, 35MM, 1/30TH AT F/2.8, ISO 200

SHOW ENVIRONMENT

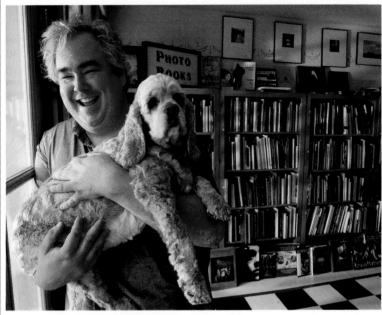

Bookshop owner, 26MM, 1/60TH AT F/6.3, ISO 125

As I've said, sometimes what someone does defines who they are. Where you situate a person in a portrait is an extension of this thinking. Your subject's home or place of work can become an effective framework for your picture. In such a setting, your subject is surrounded by familiar stuff, stuff that he or she enjoys or relies on—stuff that is important. The environment helps define who this person is for your viewer.

● So, show the environment! Not surprisingly, these kind of shots, as I mentioned in our Lens chapter, are called environmental portraits. Use the symbols available to you, the physical details, the wear and tear. This becomes your subject's stage. It also, being a familiar spot, might well serve your subject as a comfort zone. Do not criticize your kid's messy bedroom, though you might want to. Or for that matter, your crazy uncle's Mad Professor garage or workshop.

GROUPS

I don't know too many shooters out there who actually enjoy shooting groups. Let me rephrase: Most photogs I know would rather endure a short, brisk whipping than shoot a group photo.

THE RULES

Consider these Joe's rules for group portraiture:

- Move fast.
- Be confident.
- Make it fun.
- Don't be afraid to make a fool out of yourself.
- Oh, and try to use good lighting, staging, arranging and camera work.

The whole camera, lens, light deal comes at the end of these rules. Does that mean they're not important? Hardly. But I want to emphasize the unique dynamics of group portraiture.

This kind of shooting is, first and foremost, an exercise in human relations. You, the photographer, have to be authoritative but approachable. You have to be commanding but self-effacing. You have to be funny and lighthearted but you need to get things done efficiently. You have to shoot like mad, really, really fast, but pay attention to details. You have to be a lighting director, cameraperson,

Young gymnasts, 26mm, 1/160TH AT F/2.8, ISO 200

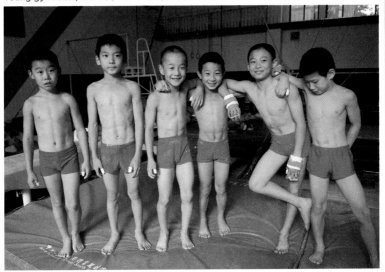

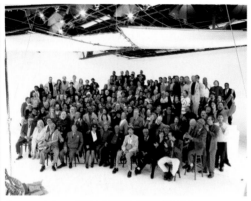

Jazz musicians, 28MM, 1/60TH AT F11, ISO 100

to have that nuclear bomb of bad light slightly overhead and behind your friends rather than in their faces.

Ask everybody to turn to the person adjacent and make final adjustments. With a big group, from back behind the lens, you can rarely see if so-and-so's tie is askew. Ask everybody to double-check and look out for his or her neighbor.

If you are using flash, try to bounce the light instead of using it straight on. If possible, get the flash (preferably *flashes*, plural) off the camera. If you use a straight flash, right from the hot shoe on the camera, and you have multiple rows of people, the first row will take the flash right in the face and heat up in your exposure. The back row won't get enough light and will also be shadowed by the light hitting the folks in the front row. So bouncing and, if possible, multiple flashes are the best way to go.

Break up your subjects' outfits! Don't let five people wearing jet black stand together. Likewise snow white. Make things irregular. Bring people with darker clothing or skin tones closer to the light source, and place people who are lighter in tone and clothing in an area where the light is not as intense. Balance the tones within the scene.

Make it fun. (I know I'm repeating myself, but it's a thought you should

set designer, social director, shrink and ringmaster.

And when the woman in the front row, the one dressed and shaped like a parade float and sporting the welder glasses that reflect all of your lights starts badgering you about how long this is going to take, you have to have the patience of Job.

Some more rules, practical ones:

Make sure all of your subjects can see the camera WITH BOTH EYES! If that guy in the last row sees the camera with one eye only, he'll likely think everything is cool, even though the person in front of him is blocking half of his face. Make people aware that both of their eyes have to see the camera. Shift accordingly.

Try to work with the existing light. If you are outside, pray for clouds. In bright overhead sun, try to put the sun behind your subjects. Though this situation is still problematic, it is better

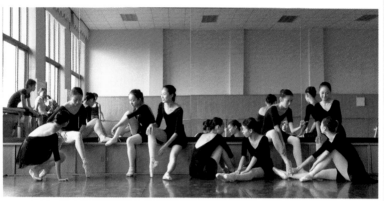

Dancers at the Beijing Dance Academy, 48MM, 1/20TH AT F/5, ISO 200

return to regularly when making group portraits.) Work as quickly as you can; you will have these folks only for minutes. Make every frame count. Project your voice, pointing right into the lens to signify that's where they need to look. Tell a joke. Kibitz. Single someone out who is loose and will respond well to banter.

Pay attention to the kids! If possible, introduce yourself and then try to REMEMBER SOME NAMES. People are surprised and inwardly pleased if you call them out personally. "Hey, Gladys, can you turn your shoulder a bit this way?" works better than, "Yo, lady in the third

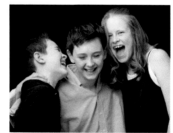

Young kids laughing during portrait shoot, 145MM, 1/250TH AT F/8, ISO 200

row in the pink outfit: Lose the hat!"

And, at the end of the process, get your group to do something exuberant. It can be in the form of a cheer or, if you are dealing with kids, maybe they can all high-five one another, hug one another, tickle one another, whatever. Let them know the picture-taking is over, and they can really go crazy.

If you lead the charge and risk being goofy; if you passionately direct the action and make it apparent that you're having fun; if you act like this . . . then your subjects will, too. In addition to following your lead, they'll also give you more time. Precious time, as all time is before the camera—you and them, making memories.

Oh, and did I mention you should make it fun?

127

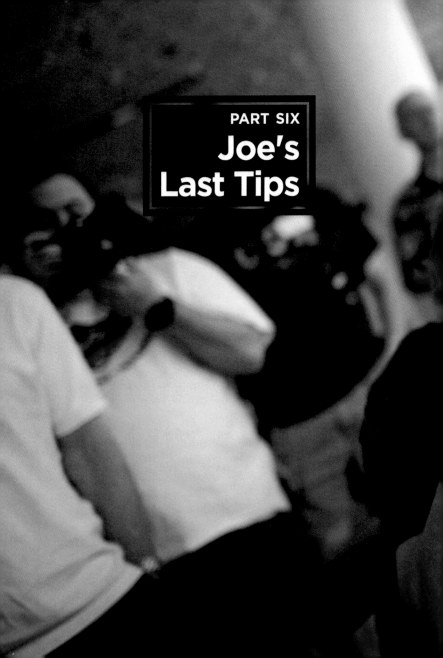

PART SIX
Joe's
Last Tips

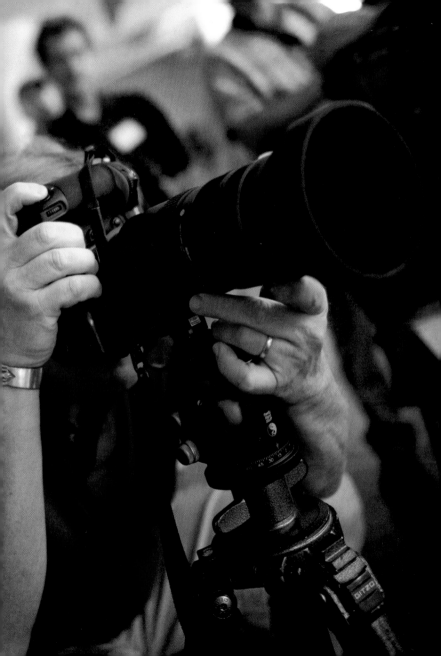

A camera is not a Fabergé egg. It is not a delicate bauble, or a museum piece to be gazed at reverently. It's a machine, a tool. Nothing more, nothing less. Now, there are those who would wax lyrical about the legendary picture creation abilities of, I don't know, some 1943 custom-built Leica rangefinder with the polished brass fittings, and the lens made of crystalline glass forged in Hephaestus's fires. Such assessments make glasses steam, grown men and women swoon and induce unbridled rapture among those who passionately worship at the altar of gear.

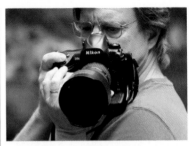

I support the camera on my left shoulder.

● These people are generally called collectors. Photographers, they ain't—not usually.

What best sums up my feelings about cameras came from legendary war photographer Don McCullin. He said, "I only use a camera like I use a toothbrush. It does the job." Amen.

My first motor-driven camera was a Nikon F, with a detachable base plate filled with batteries. It was rugged and heavy, a great street camera. Marty Forscher, the legendary wizard of Professional Camera Repair on 47th Street in Manhattan, used to tell me, "You could hammer a nail with that camera!" Of course, he then urged me not to do that.

Maybe it was these beginnings, working with a metal monster of a camera, that first taught me the necessity of holding my cameras

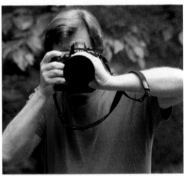

My arms are not helping to support the camera here.

steady. Or, it could have been my workaday beginnings as a newspaper grunt, where the only thing you gripped tighter than the camera and lens was the beer bottle at the end of your shift.

And conversely, perhaps it is the current gloss of computerized technology that has draped itself over all things photographic that has folks new to the game holding these machines

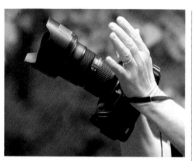

I loop the camera strap around my wrist.

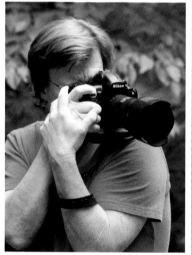

Double grip for super-slow shutter speeds

moments behind the lens, something perhaps embedded in your genes. I never thought about why, but from the first I put the camera to my left eye.

This, oddly enough, gave me an advantage in terms of holding cameras steady, even at slow speeds. (Right-eyed folks, keep reading, there are tips in here for you, too.)

Because of this quirk, the choice of left eye, I am able to bring my left side into play, leading with my left leg, assuming what is basically a boxer's stance. My left shoulder swings forward and slightly down, becoming a platform for the bottom of my camera to rest and stabilize against. The eyepiece goes directly to my eye, with my brow making contact with the prism head of the camera. My right hand grips the machine, index finger at the ready. My elbows tuck in to my sides and my left hand comes under the lens, where it supports whatever length of glass is attached to the camera. Exhale. Concentrate. Shoot.

Let's take the setup in steps.

I feel genuinely naked if my camera strap isn't looped around my left wrist when I prepare to look through a lens.

My left foot moves forward, bringing with it my left shoulder. (This move has an additional benefit in that my center of gravity is now more squarely under the camera.)

The camera rests there, on my shoulder, and my left hand comes under the barrel of the lens. It does not go over, or on top of the lens. In the photo opposite below, look at where my elbow would go if I placed my left

delicately, gently, like a magic box inside which the pixels gambol about like tiny woodland creatures.

Let's talk technique. Pick the camera up. Which eye do you bring it to? This will come naturally, something you do from the very first

131

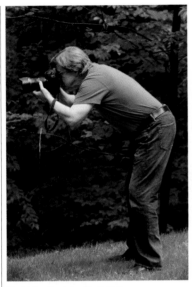

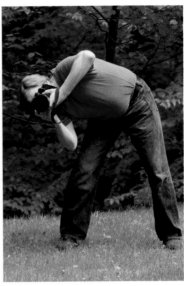

Bad idea for how to stand

Worse idea for how to stand

hand over the barrel. Two very bad things occur: My left arm, instead of supporting the whole deal, is out there flapping around like a chicken wing. And, with my hand on top of the lens, I'm actually increasing the weight I have to support. Not good.

Right-eyed shooters: You can do a modified version of my holding technique. Though the use of your right eye negates the support of the left shoulder, the basics remain the same. You grip with your right hand and support with the left. This brings both of your elbows into your sides. Now your body and arms are fully joined in support of the camera. Also, when you want to shoot vertical, rotate

the camera, not your body. I see this mistake made all the time.

I mentioned center of gravity. Get it under the camera. Don't bend over or twist. A bad camera posture is a surefire ticket to chronic back pain and the chiropractor's office. If you are uncomfortable out there, your pictures will suffer because (a) you can't concentrate, and (b) you will be fatigued.

I can't emphasize enough the negative effect fatigue has on your picture-making abilities. If you are exhausted, if you're carrying too much gear and you're not holding your camera with ease and efficiency, that latte and the chocolate scone down the block at Starbuck's look mighty tempting. You begin to rationalize bad behaviors. Ahh, the light's not so great. I'll come back out later. Let's eat!

Economy of movement and handling the right amount of gear well extends your field time and your patience behind the lens. These basics just allow you to have more fun. It's all good.

Now, your camera is properly at your eye. Relax. Exhale. Don't jab the shutter button. Squeeze it gently. Some folks advocate actually rolling your finger over the shutter release. That's fine. Discover what suits you. Just don't hit the shutter button like you're playing Frogger at a video arcade.

And remember this: Your first frame may (and I say may) have a tendency to be your least sharp. You're excited, maybe you saw something quick and you're trying to get the snap before the little kid bouncing the ball disappears around the corner, and you jab the shutter. That initial, kinetic impulse you impart to the button may be a touch more jagged than your subsequent clicks, when your head and eye are, quite probably, more fully engaged and the camera is truly nestled in your hands. This isn't always the case, but it's something to be aware of.

Strategies for low-light shooting: Take everything I mention above, and add to them. Shift your camera off single advance to consecutive high. This will allow you to burst the camera. When you burst the camera, you increase your chances that one or more (with luck, many more) frames will be sharp. This would not apply, say, to a picture you might be making of a rock

formation—something that does not move or talk back to you. But this is very handy when dealing with those most mercurial of subjects, people.

Another tip: See where my left hand is in the photo on the bottom of page 131? It is crossed over my body and is clapped over my right, or camera-grip, hand. I employ this technique when I am feeling really skinny on shutter speed, when the shutter is set dangerously low and I know shooting this picture sharp is roughly akin to playing craps in Vegas. This double grip allows me to almost fold myself around the camera and lens. I don't need my left hand to focus the lens; the camera is doing that for me. I set my zoom where I want it, so I don't need adjustment there. I am free to use my somewhat functionless left hand as further stabilization. (Note: I never use this technique when I am using truly long glass. When the lens gets long, my left hand stays with it, underneath, cradling and supporting it.)

You never knew just getting your camera to your eye was an athletic event, did you? But there's a reason for the gymnastics: Sharpness is crucial. So is quality. Quality, as we know by now, is linked to keeping your ISO low, not bouncing it up to stratospheric numbers. Keeping your ISO low (or moderate) can lead you into the challenge of holding your camera at shutter speeds that are lower than most of the manuals recommend.

Once again, this late in the game, you are breaking the rules. Good for you.

One of the best pieces of advice I can offer about walking around with cameras and lenses is: Look like you're not. And I'm not necessarily talking about extreme environments, in which there's risk associated with just taking a stroll, much less taking a stroll looking like an ambulatory promotion for Adorama Camera superstore. I'm talking about every day.

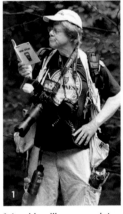

1. Looking like a complete newbie and an easy target

● I could be talking about the local county fair or weekend carnival or farmer's market. Your photo shoot could be down the block, or it could be a place at the far reaches of several oceans. If you want your pictures to appear natural, unforced and unposed, blending in is the key. Even at the family picnic, you don't want the kids to worry that there's a picture-taker at work. The last thing you need to do is strut about, chest and limbs bristling with high-priced digital hardware. It draws attention when you don't want any. Hang a couple of cameras around your neck with appropriately gaudy manufacturer's logos all over the straps and that nifty vest from Orvis, the one with 33 pockets you now feel the need to fill with bits and pieces of photog junk—well, you might as well hang a cow bell around your neck. You're going to make everyone uneasy. Even your kid.

When taking travel photographs, for example, most times you are going to be eyeballed as a fish out of water. You should try to not be a strange-looking fish on top of that.

So think about the kind of pictures you want from this particular adventure. Are you envisioning environmental portraits, street scenes, cultural details? Will you be entering places of religious observance, where the premium will be on quiet and unobtrusive reverence as you make pictures? Or is the order of the day a double-decker tour bus where you'll have to reach into crowds and scenes without being right there on street level with the action?

Previsualize, in other words. Plan carefully. For street photography, do you have a small phrase book and a map that can that can be tucked away? Sunglasses, sunblock, Ibuprofen, the phone number of the hotel? Identification? Cell phone? One that has GPS that before you left home you programmed to include the area of the world in which you will be wandering about?

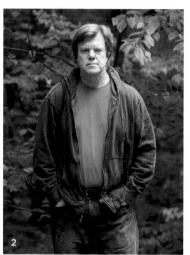
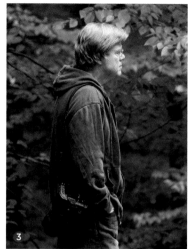

2. Trying to look inconspicuous ... 3. Walking with my camera slung over my shoulder

These things can fit into a cargo pocket of your pants or shorts, or a very small, nondescript fanny pack. Your camera and lens, of course, are going to be bulkier. I urge you, if you're in any kind of exotic locale, to avoid working with a digital camera hanging around your neck. It will flop about your chest as you walk, and it's a certain "I'm a tourist" giveaway. It is also a possible quick trip to the emergency room if someone tries to snatch it, and it wrenches or wraps around your neck. (Don't laugh. I once had a colleague who worked in a country where street thieves were so adept at slashing handbag and camera straps with razors and making off with the goods that my friend had his leather camera straps replaced with bicycle chains.)

I advocate, for most adventurous meanders, one camera and one lens. Zoom lenses are terrific for this mildly covert mission you have engaged in. If you are up close, a 24–70mm or a 24–85mm zoom is perfect. For longer work, 70–200 or 70–300 would work out fine. For the ambitious, who really wish to push their skills, prime, fast lenses that we spoke of earlier are wonderful environmental, scene-setting, "street" lenses.

Once you have decided how little, or how much gear you are going to tote, carrying becomes yet another matter for discussion. I have managed to stay at least somewhat inconspicuous by slinging a nondesigner strap over my shoulder and letting the lens (particularly a longer lens) rest behind

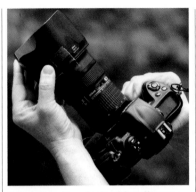

Secure your lens shade with gaffer tape to help keep it on.

me, on my backside. Whichever shoulder I use, I generally keep the corresponding hand in a pocket, so I maintain contact with the rig and keep it close to my body. Occasionally, I even take my other hand, wrap it slightly behind me and keep contact with the lens this way, too. I'm at least not walking around with a blinking neon sign on my forehead saying, "I'm Not From Around Here."

Another tip: Lens shades. Use 'em. The lens shade protects the front element of the lens to a degree, but, more important, it prevents light scatter from dancing across the glass surface of the lens and fraying at your photograph's contrast. (Any sharp, hard light that flares right into the lens, or even hits the front element at an unfortunate angle, will potentially degrade the image quality. The lens shade will help prevent this.)

Now, my experience is that most lens shades offered by most camera manufacturers are cheeseball pieces of junk. Plastic, with plastic mounts, they are primed, when they bump into stuff, to pop off your lens and clatter onto the floor—a bad move at Midnight Mass.

To prevent this, I take small pieces of gaffer tape and leave them attached to the lens shade. Then when you affix the shade to the lens, just wad the gaffer tape into the seam between the two. The shade will stay on now.

To effectively observe a scene, don't make a scene.

JOE'S LAST TIP

THE LAST OF THE LAST TIPS:
- ❏ Shoot early.
- ❏ Shoot often.
- ❏ Shoot the stuff you love.

And, oh yeah, have I mentioned yet . . . HAVE FUN!

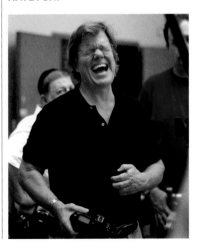

Have you ever gone to a party at a neighbor's house and become part of a conversation that veers into terminology and turf you don't understand? Folks around you become engrossed by a certain arcane subject, while the half-smile freezes on your face, your head actively nods like a bobblehead doll's, and your eyes desperately search for the next passing hors d'oeuvre tray. The conversationalists might not even be mean-spirited or trying to prove they're superior, they just don't have the time or desire to school you on the lingo, bring you up to speed on the topic at hand.

This book is not that conversation. It has been designed, we hope, to be user-friendly and build photo skills from the ground up. To that end, we're going to collect here a bunch of terms and definitions, many of which will be reiterative if you've just finished our six chapters, some of which you will encounter in your camera's manual. I'll also share some field terminology, the tribal language of shooters everywhere. A glossary is a good place: a safe harbor to which you can retreat if the waters are getting choppy. Whenever you want a refresher or feel unsure about a certain topic, come on back here for support.

Let's get started. Alphabetical fashion works best.

AF-assist illuminator. A beam of light the camera sprays onto the subject to help itself achieve focus in very dim conditions. Depending on the model and how you have your camera programmed, the AF-assist illuminator can activate automatically in low light. It will not be seen in the actual photo, though, because it shuts down as soon as the picture starts to be taken. The AF-assist illuminator is useful in low-light situations in which a camera's autofocus feature needs a helping hand. The "AF" in the name stands for "autofocus." *See* autofocus.

aperture. An adjustable circular opening inside the lens that regulates how much light transits the lens and hits the sensor. It is basically a hole in the lens that you can control by making it bigger or smaller. A small hole allows very little light to reach the sensor; a big hole allows a great deal of light to pour through.

artificial light. Light from sources other than the sun; usually refers to studio lighting or any interior or man-made lighting. Unlike sunlight, which tends to be relatively calm in terms of its color (warm, cool, neutral) the many sources of artificial light give the color wheel a good spin and can present themselves to your digital camera as various shades of funky. Get used to that, and be prepared to experiment with your camera's white-balance settings in response to things like cityscapes, building interiors and the like.

aspect ratio. The ratio of a picture's length to its width. Digital images typically have an aspect ratio of 4:3. Old 35mm film has an aspect ratio of 3:2.

autofocus. A camera feature that allows it to focus automatically. Autofocus systems consist of sensors that communicate with motors in the lens that lock on to a scene and snap the lens into sharp focus. There are camera models that have a "tracking" feature in which the camera will lock on to a moving subject and retain focus even as the subject moves. Autofocus effectiveness is highly dependent on the quality and quantity of light. In very dim situations, when the light lacks contrast, autofocus systems suffer, slow down or misjudge. Virtually all of today's digital cameras can focus automatically, which in the past was the task—the responsibility—of the picture-taker.

available light. Existing light surrounding a subject, not added by the photographer. Can be artificial or natural. Also called ambient light or existing light. Famous LIFE shooter Gene Smith, who paid no attention to textbook definitions, once defined his version of available light as "any *$%#@ light that's available." He used the sun, flash, flashlights, streetlights, you name it. And Smith made great pictures with his "available light," which was not nature's.

backlighting. Light originating behind a subject. Good for drama, but sometimes tough to meter effectively. When you are shooting a seriously

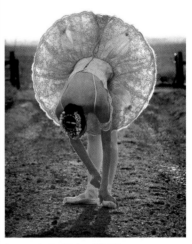

Image shot with backlighting

backlit subject, you are breaking a time-honored rule: Shoot with the light, or shoot with the sun at your back. With backlighting, you shoot directly into a strong source of light. Backlighting calls for experimentation and bracketing. *See* bracketing.

black card. A piece of black foam board, cardboard or anything else matte, black and non-reflective used to manipulate shots that require long exposures, such as fireworks.

blown-out. A term used to describe the highlight area of an image when the exposure causes the highlights to appear pure white with no detail. Highlight heaven. Be careful! Blown-out areas of your picture can be really cool-looking, or just areas of devastation. These areas live at the right-hand side of the histogram, which I refer to as Ice Planet 255, where there is no sustainable pixel life.

bouncing light. The process by which a photographer takes existing light and redirects it via a reflector or "bounce board." Can have the effect of "filling in" shadows or dark areas. Also refers to the process of taking artificial light, such as flash, and instead of using it in direct, harsh fashion, "bouncing," or reflecting, the flash off a ceiling or wall, thus making it softer and more natural-looking.

bracketing. The process of shooting what is presumed to be the right exposure for a frame and then safeguarding yourself by shooting at least two additional exposures, one on either side of that "right" one, underexposing one and overexposing the other. This is highly recommended for static subjects, such as rocks, flowers and mountains. People, well, people move, right? They change expression. Your kid gets handed the "Eighth-Grader of the Year" award only once. So bracketing in these fluid, moment-to-moment situations is dicey. You don't want the moment to be recorded on a bad or off bracket. So, when the chips are down and you have to get that shot, try to make sure you have dialed in the correct exposure, and be ready to make it. If timing isn't the key factor of your approach and success, by all means shoot up and down the exposure scale. It will not only ensure success for that particular shot, it will also make you increasingly familiar with how the digital camera sensor performs in different lighting

and exposure scenarios. Bracketing is education.

A subset of bracketing is **autobracketing.** This is a feature available on most DSLRs that you can program to automatically sweep through an entire range of exposures, one after another. You can dictate how many shots and the extent of over- and underexposure. This is very popular now with the folks who play with HDR (high dynamic range). *See* high dynamic range.

bulb (shutter speed "B"). A shutter speed dial selection that keeps the shutter open as long as you keep the shutter button depressed. Essential for nighttime shooting. Its name comes from the old days when the shutter on some cameras was activated by squeezing a bulb and then releasing it.

camera buffer. This is a holding pen, if you will, for the electronic, digitized information you just shot as that info moves from your camera to your memory card. Cameras and memory cards have a thing called "write speed" that, without getting too techy, is basically the speed at which all this precious picture information is transferred. Your rate of shooting pictures will almost certainly, on occasion, outstrip the speed at which the digital data is moved from the camera to the card. This is where the buffer comes into play. The more expensive the camera, the bigger the buffer and the more pictures you can shoot before your camera cries, "¡No más!" and locks you out. If you are frantically punching the button while your kid is blowing out the candles, and the camera is not taking pictures, you probably overshot the buffer. Most cameras will hold anywhere from 5 to 25 files in the buffer. High-end camera models hold a lot more than moderate or basic models. (It, of course, depends on the size of the file you are shooting. Raw files, being larger, will fill up your buffer more quickly than basic JPEGs.) If you are locked out, it really just means waiting a few seconds (or a few dozen seconds) to let the camera recover and clear the buffer, which allows you to once again rip through frames.

camera obscura. Basically, an optical device, usually a box with a lens adapted on a hole, that projects an inverted image of the outside view. In the early 1800s, French photo pioneer Nicéphore Niépce began using a camera obscura with photosensitive material inside to produce what is generally acknowledged as the first photographic image. I occasionally use this term to describe some of the work I currently see.

camera shake. Movement of a camera when the exposure is being made that results in a blurred or unsharp image, especially at slow shutter speeds. Shaking hands, unsteady tripods and surrounding vibration can all cause camera shake. How much camera shake, or blurriness, you inflict on your picture can often relate to how many cups of espresso you've consumed.

catchlight. The reflection of a light in your subject's eyes. A tiny spectral highlight that sparks the eyes and creates a bit of drama. It

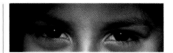
Catchlight reflected in the eyes

often directly reflects the source of light, such as a window or a flash. Currently, catchlights, always just a bit of a given, are the subject of much discussion among photogs. Some like catchlights, others don't. There is a lot of postproduction going on nowadays, so these little splashes of light are now often altered or eliminated. My opinion? Let the catchlights roll. They are what they are.

chimping. Looking at each frame right after shooting it. *Click, click, click! Ooh, ooh, ooh!* This practice originated with the LCD. It reflects the compulsive, absolute need on the part of many shooters to check out the picture they just shot. Be careful with this. It is a distraction. The best picture may be occurring while you are looking at the last one. You'll have more time to truly contemplate results—and to learn—later.

closeup. A picture of a subject that fills the frame. Most of your human subjects will object to their closeups. Flowers? Go for it. They can't complain about it. For that matter, neither can your dog.

composition. The arrangement of the elements of a scene within the background, middle ground and foreground. Very important.

contrast. Refers to quality of light and how quickly a scene rotates from bright highlight into black. A sudden, sharp change from light to black—high contrast. Gradual—medium contrast. Almost no change—low contrast. Photogs describe these conditions in very colorful terms, many of them unprintable, depending on how the light suits their assignment and if it is good to work with at that moment.

crop factor. This is all about sensor size. There are many DSLR cameras available now that have a full-frame sensor, which is very close to the dimensions of the 35mm film camera. But there are also lots of models that have a smaller sensor, which produces a "crop," or "crop factor." The image will appear magnified, but it is really not. It is simply the smaller sensor at work, taking a smaller piece of the scene.

cropping. Removing parts of an image's edges in order to improve the composition. Cropping means that when you had your camera to your eye, you were constrained and couldn't move or you had the wrong lens on or you were just plain lazy. Cropping *in* the camera is vastly preferable to post-click cropping at your computer. Cropping after the fact means that your picture is on the operating table, and you, no longer the *artiste*, are now a surgeon, determining how to painfully save this patient.

dedicated flash. An electronic flash unit, designed to work with a specific model of camera, that integrates with the camera's exposure meter and exposure controls to allow the fully automatic use of the flash.

depth of field (DOF). The range of distance in a scene that appears to be in focus—it's basically what is sharp in the picture. By that I mean acceptably sharp, which stops short of critically sharp. In portraiture, for instance, critical sharpness should fall right at someone's eyes, whereas the shoulder or the tip of the nose could be acceptably sharp, i.e., within depth of field. DOF will vary according to how close the camera is to the subject, the millimeter length of the lens and the aperture opening of the lens. Quick hints on DOF: A long lens, wide aperture and close proximity to the subject will yield a very shallow depth of field. Shorter lenses, narrow or small aperture and a bit of distance to the subject will increase the depth of field. Getting to know how much or how little depth of field individual picture scenarios require is just a matter of practice and time behind the lens.

diaphragm. An adjustable set of overlapping, movable metal blades (usually six or seven but can be as few as five or as many as nine) inside a lens that determines the amount of light entering a camera. The diaphragm controls the size of the hole, or aperture, thereby permitting more or less light to pass through the lens to the viewfinder.

diffuser. A light softener. Ever see the effect of a naked incandescent bulb in a lamp? Hard shadows, tough to look at. Put a lamp shade on. Ah, that's better. You have just diffused the light. There are many types of diffusers on sale in the photo marketplace. There are also ad hoc diffusers around the house—a white handkerchief, white bedsheets or pillowcases, vellum or tracing paper, a piece of copier paper, a window curtain. Just about anything that transmits and spreads light and has no color to it can, in a pinch, be used as a diffuser.

digital single-lens reflex (DSLR) camera. A digital camera with only one lens for both viewing and picture-taking. In both film and digital versions of SLR cameras, an image is reflected onto a viewing screen by a movable mirror inside the camera. The mirror flips out of the way just before the shutter opens, allowing light to strike the film or sensor.

diopter. Eyeglasses for your camera. Many models have a little button right by the eyepiece that you can adjust for your eye. Helpful for us older folks.

distortion. Refers to what occurs from using certain kinds of lenses. Wide lenses produce "distortion" when they are used close to a subject (a relatively normal nose suddenly looks like a ballistic missile) or pointed around at extreme angles (otherwise straight buildings look like they are about to topple over). Long lenses produce compression, which is a type of distortion that "stacks up," or compresses, a scene. (Think of telephoto shots down a busy Manhattan avenue. The hundreds of people actually out there walking all of a sudden look like thousands because the long-lens perspective squashes them all together.) This type of lens-based distortion is either purposeful and has graphic intent that assists the photo, or it is just plain bad camera work—the result of careless or inappropriate lens use.

And there is lens distortion of the technical sort, which relates to certain lenses and their construction. There are two major types of distortion: **Barrel distortion,** which is present in small amounts in some wide-angle lenses and very noticeably in fish-eye lenses. Here, the straight lines near the edges of the frame bow outward from the center to form a barrel shape. With **pincushion distortion,** which is present in small amounts in some telephoto lenses, the straight lines near the edges of the frame bend in toward the center to resemble the sides of a pincushion. These lens aberrations obviously occur more often in the all-purpose, zoom-it-from-here-to-there cheaper lens options. Better lenses, with good glass and good construction, will skirt most distortion issues.

EV button. A button that allows you to adjust the exposure up or down, according to your taste, even when the camera is in an automatic metering mode. The camera will often look at a scene and be unduly influenced by big areas of shadows or highlights. It can be fooled, in other words, and yield a bad or incorrect exposure. You can correct for this in manual mode by changing either your shutter speed or your f-stop. In an automatic exposure mode, the way to alter the camera's exposure reaction is to use this button, generally located in a handy position near the shutter button itself. *See* exposure value.

exposure. This is basically how much light hits the sensor. You'll hear the terms "bad exposure" and "good exposure" as long as you shoot. With practice, you'll produce more of the latter. Generally, the exposure is described by the time it took to make it. "That was a two-second exposure." To further refine and describe the shot, you can add in the f-stop that was used. "I shot that at 1/60th at f/5.6."

exposure value (EV). Denotes all combinations of a camera's shutter speed and aperture that give the same exposure. The proper exposure value for any given scene is the one you think looks best. EV is arrived at by determining the appropriate f-stop and shutter speed combination. The choices you make for the "appropriate" specific shutter speeds and aperture openings will often be determined in reaction to your subject matter. For example, shooting a horse race will require a fast shutter speed, which will in turn influence your choice of f-stop. A majestic landscape may be better shot with lots of depth of field, resulting in the selection of a small f-stop, around f/16 or so. That will pretty much dictate that your shutter speed be somewhat slow, which will then require you to use a tripod. All of this photo *stuff* is, as you can see, interrelated and will become more intuitive as you practice regularly.

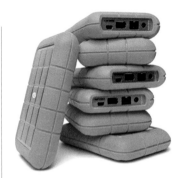

External hard drives

external hard drive. A small, portable storage device for digital information. As your picture-making prowess increases, you will take more and more pictures worth saving, requiring more and more digital storage space. These small, affordable hard drives are a good solution for storing all of this newly minted digital information. If you try storing all of the photos on your laptop or home computer, it will slow down and eventually fill up, and then give up. An external hard drive, able to connect to your computer via cables, is the answer. Though physically small, they can store lots of ones and zeroes. (There are drives now out there that can store two terrabytes [2TB] and still fit in your pocket.) External hard drives are just about essential now because the higher-end digital cameras are producing larger and larger files. They have to be put somewhere. (And they have to be backed up! So don't put all your stuff on just one drive. If there is a given about hard drives, it is that they will eventually fail! So storage on multiple drives is a good strategy.)

field of view. The area of a scene that a lens sees. This is determined by focal length: A wide-angle lens, which has a short focal length, sees more of a scene than a telephoto lens, which has a long focal length. Also called *angle of view*.

fill flash. A light source that illuminates an area of a photograph that would otherwise be too dark. The operative word here is fill, which connotes the fact that the resulting exposure is a mix of the ambient conditions "filled" or assisted by a source of artificial light, i.e., a flash. A full-out flash exposure looks and feels different from a fill-flash exposure.

film speed. The measure of how sensitive the film is, or how quickly it can react to light, often quantified as its ISO (International Organization for Standardization) number. Film speed is particular to the type of film you use—if you're still using film—and is not changeable with the flick of a button, the way ISO can be changed in today's digital cameras. *See* ISO.

fish-eye lens. A wide lens that generally has a coverage of about 180 degrees. It is très cool to use selectively, but with that superwide view comes something that needs to be managed carefully—distortion. Try shooting somebody's portrait with this type of lens and you'll quickly see why it's called a fish-eye. *See* distortion.

flare. Uncontrolled or powerful light hitting the lens at a bad angle and creating a very bright spot or lines in your photograph is called flare. Point a wide-angle lens at the sun, and you'll find out about flare. Flare is not always a bad thing, but it's generally a wise idea to avoid it in most instances. Use lens shades! They will generally help control flare. Specifically, if you want to employ flare in your composition, ask yourself before clicking: Why? And now, how? *See* lens shade.

flash. A light source used to produce instantaneous illumination on the subject of a photograph. Many cameras have built-in flashes, but separate flashes are also available, often referred to as "hot-shoe flashes" or "speed lights." These external flashes offer the photographer great creative freedom in the way the flash light interacts with the subject. They are also the source of great terror among new camera users, given the split-second, apparently uncontrollable burst of light that attends flash photography. Relax. Flash is—or certainly can be—your friend.

flash sync speed. This refers to the speed at which the flash will synchronize with a shutter speed of your choosing. When using a flash, you have to coordinate it with the action of opening the shutter to get its full exposure effect. This can be pretty straightforward at mid-range or low shutter speeds, but it is a crucial thing to pay attention to at higher shutter speeds. In most cameras, the upper limit of proper sync is around 1/200th or 1/250th of a second. Go above this, and you will start getting dark or underexposed frames, meaning the shutter opened and closed too quickly to get all of the flash. There are high-speed flash modes available in certain cameras that allow flash operation at extremely high shutter speeds. Read the manual about these modes.

flat light. A quality of light that is lifeless and has just about zero contrast. Often associated with heavy cloud cover.

focus cursors. These are movable little doobers in your viewfinder that direct the sensitivity of the autofocus system right to where you want it to go, presumably the area of critical focus in your picture. With different camera models, there is a thumb pad or a wheel in the back of the camera that enables you to move them around. Be careful with them! Read the manual. There are different types of autofocus systems. Some enable one point of focus, which is represented by that glowing cursor. Other modes enable a group of cursors, all of which are sensitized. Still others activate the entire field of potential autofocus coverage and have features such as "lock on" for moving subjects and face recognition. Each of these requires experimentation, so that you learn which one suits particular scenes or subjects. Point-and-shoot cameras often offer focus options, such as "landscape" and "portrait." *See* autofocus.

frame. The extent of the picture, including the subject, foreground and background. When you put your eye to the viewfinder, you are "framing" your picture.

frames per second (FPS). Describes how fast you can take pictures. There are cameras on the market that will fire really fast, making as many as eight or nine pictures per second. Other cameras, depending on type and price, move quite a bit slower than that. A fast frame rate is handy for shooting sports, of course, and any other fast-moving subject. You can regulate the frame rate by dialing in single or consecutive modes on your camera. Some will have three choices—low, moderate and fast advance. Fast is the noise you hear in the background of all of the movie scenes in which there are photographers milling about, trying to get a picture of the politician or the perpetrator. It sounds exciting at the cinema, but be careful: Fast advance can fill up your memory card mighty fast, giving you a new challenge to solve.

f-stop. The clicks on the aperture dial that open and close the diaphragm blades of the lens. Among the most common f-stops are f/2.8, f/4, f/5.6, f/8, f/11 and f/16. These are "full" stops of light. As you can see, each f-stop number is approximately 1.4 times larger than the one preceding it, and each full click from one stop to the next either doubles the light going through the lens or cuts it in half, depending on which way you are clicking. The smaller numbers, somewhat counterintuitively, denote the larger lens openings. Conversely, the larger the f-number, the smaller the lens opening. Also called *f-number*.

gaffer tape. A heavy-duty photographer's tape that is easily removed. Not to be confused with duct tape. If you want to induce the ire of your subject and have no desire to be invited back to the home/location/executive suite you have just been photographing in, use duct tape, which leaves a sticky residue or outright pulls away the surface of whatever it has been stuck to. Duct tape will remove paint, wallpaper—you name it. Gaffer tape is movie tape, really. A bit pricey at the camera store, but worth it because, although it is strong, it will generally not do damage to whatever you apply it to.

Also, in a pinch, it will be a quick fix for your camera, tripod, lights, battery packs, stands and just about anything else on a shoot. There's literally nothing on location that can't be made better by an application of gaffer tape. The world of photography spins on this particularly sticky item.

glass. Photog slang for "lens." The term *fast glass* refers to lenses with wide aperture possibilities. *Long glass* refers to telephoto lenses, usually starting around 135mm and up. *Wide glass* refers to wide-angle lenses, used for a scene-setting type of picture, which shows a lot of the environment. *Bad glass* describes cheap, slow or unsharp lenses. As in, "They couldn't make a decent ashtray out of the glass in this lens." (These are the second-rate lenses often seen advertised in the backs of the photo mags. If a lens seems too good to be true at the advertised price, it generally is.)

gray card. Literally, a gray card. Photographers sometimes use gray cards as targets to ensure a consistent exposure or to correct the white balance of their photographs. Photographers who use this type of assist in determining an exposure are generally studio shooters, or outright control freaks. Ever see a gray card out there on the 50-yard line or in the middle of a street riot?

hard lighting. Bright, intense light that causes sharp, dark shadows.

high dynamic range (HDR). A process in which shooters take numerous different exposures of the same thing, and then, in post-processing, combine them all into one picture. Again, this is not recommended so much for people photography. (Those darn people! Why won't they just stay put!) But when presented with a static subject, such as a landscape, this can be a very effective tactic to expand the camera sensor's dynamic range, which is limited. It should be said: The ease and current popularity of this technique has prompted many picture-takers to shoot subject matter that should have been left alone.

highlight. The brighter areas of a photo, which are sometimes tough to control. A "blown" highlight refers to an area in the photo that has no detail and is not recoverable in postproduction. Blown highlights are generally not desirable, but then again, depending on the aspiration, could be really striking (think certain kinds of fashion photos). Most often, though, an out-of-control

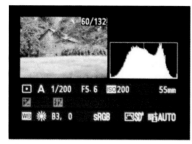

Histogram, upper right, on camera LCD

highlight in someone's glasses, or right smack in the middle of a forehead, is not a good thing.

histogram. A graph of the shadow-to-highlight va lues of a picture. As is true with graphs in general, a histogram is pretty boring but can provide useful information, taken in proper doses. Some shooters are slaves to the histogram. Others don't give a hoot. I tend to be in the latter category. In a histogram, black is 0 and dead white is 255. In the middle, not surprisingly, live all the more moderate tonalities. Understandably, the camera's meter, which I tend to think of as a bit of a herd animal, likes to cluster in the middle, never foraying out to the edges where bad stuff could happen. The middle of the histogram is safe and reproducible. A classic histogram looks a bit like a bell curve, with a lot of values right there in the middle, tapering to the ends or extremes. Yet, a lot of interesting photos are out there on the edges. So use the histogram as it was intended—an informational guideline, not the holy grail of exposure.

hot shoe. A slotted bracket that connects an external flash or other device to the camera, located atop the viewing prism, or viewfinder, just above where you look through the camera. The hot shoe provides an electrical connection (hence the word hot) between a flash (or other accessory, such as a radio-remote flash controller) and the camera. There's so much to be said about what a hot shoe can do, well, there's a book's worth of material. At least I thought so, when I wrote *The Hot Shoe Diaries.* Hope you like it.

ISO. Refers to the sensitivity of the chip, or sensor, and expresses in numeric fashion the "speed" at which the sensor will accept light. Obviously, high ISO numbers, such as 1600, will enable photography in low-light conditions. In bright sun, ISO 100 or 200 is plenty. "ISO" comes from International Organization for Standardization.

JPEG. Also referred to as "jpg" (pronounced "jay peg"), this is a very popular file format for digital photographs. Other formats are available, such as TIFF, but JPEG and raw are by far the most popular. Think of the difference between these two this way: The raw file is the block of unshaped marble that comes out of the camera relatively untouched, to be sculpted later, by you, in the computer, using the miracles of post-processing. The JPEG comes out of the camera already chiseled and shaped. All that extra stone is already gone forever. You can make some fairly minor alterations at this point, but the basic work of crafting the file is done in the camera. In some ways, because a JPEG is a finished file in the camera, it forces you to get everything right at the moment of exposure.

The raw file generated by the camera has lots more potential information than the JPEG. The JPEG is "compressed" in the camera. It is a smaller file and a highly efficient way to shoot. But, because it is a relatively done deal, packaged and compressed in the camera, it does not carry with it nearly the color information and post-processing possibilities the raw file does. With the raw file, if you make a mistake, you have a good shot at correcting that after the fact. (For instance, imagine shooting outdoors all day with the white balance set for indoor lighting. All your pictures have an off-color cast. With raw files, you can, in postproduction, redirect the white balance to the proper color cast or color temperature with a click of a button. That's not possible with a JPEG. It is what it is, and the possibilities to reshape it after a shoot are far more limited.) JPEG, by the way, is an acronym for "Joint Photographic Experts Group." They meet every month and compress files. A wild bunch indeed.

Kelvin temperature. The temperature of light. Named after Lord Kelvin, it is a scale that calls out various types of light in degrees, or degrees Kelvin. Normal daylight is generally around 5,600 K. Tungsten or incandescent pulls in about 3,400 K. The lower on the scale, the warmer or more red the light; the higher, the more blueish in cast. Remember it this way: By going up in Kelvin, you're heading to heaven and blue sky. The lower the Kelvin, the more probable that your picture's headed straight to the red fires of hell.

lens shade. An accessory affixed to the end of the lens, used to reduce glare and prevent lens flare. Generally made of plastic or rubber, a lens shade can look like a simple cone that either screws or bayonets on to the front element of the lens. Some are more complex shapes, known as "flower," or "tulip" hoods. These are cut in an irregular shape so they don't compromise the view of zoom lenses as the angle of view changes or widens. Also known as a lens hood. *See* flare.

lens-stabilizing system. These are lenses that, by pushing or sliding a button on the lens itself, can engage an onboard system of stabilization to combat camera shake. There are specific moves being made in the lens, but just think of this as a gyroscopelike device inside the lens that helps you hold it steady. In the early days of these lenses, it was always advisable to turn off the gyro systems when mounting the camera or lens to a tripod. Now, many models automatically sense the stability of a tripod and shut themselves off. The biggest dogs among many in the camera world are Nikon and Canon. Nikon calls its system VR, for "vibration reduction." Canon calls its version IS, for "image stabilization." I'm sure there are other

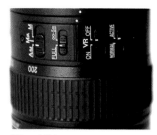

Nikon VR lens

names out there. Also please note: With point-and-shoot cameras, the stabilization is often activated in the camera, not the lens.

liquid crystal display (LCD). This is the little hi-def TV on the back of your camera. It possesses the strange power of a Lay's potato chip: Once you start looking at it, you can't stop. For good reason. It is an excellent way to check your sharpness, see the frame and make some quick field judgments about what to shoot next. As everyone counsels, it is not a great way to judge exposure. The LCD is very limited, and what looks good there might not look so good when you launch the image back at your computer. Yet, there isn't a shooter I know who doesn't keep tabs on his or her ballpark exposure by glancing at the LCD.

In many camera models, the brightness of the LCD is adjustable. Try to fine-tune it so that it looks close to what your files look like back at the home computer. If it is way too bright, for instance, it may push you to underexpose your images, which may make for an unpleasant surprise later when you try to work the files.

live view. A way to compose your photograph without putting your eye to the viewfinder. In this mode, you actually preview the shot you are about to make on the LCD. The camera's image sensor bypasses the mirror (which reflects the image up to the viewfinder) and sends the view the lens sees directly to the electronic display at the back of the camera. Most point-and-shoot cameras operate this way, but now many newer DSLRs offer this as an option.

macro lens. Lens optimized for close work. There are different millimeter ranges that work best for certain types of subject matter, but generally macro lenses have really close-in focusing distances. Really good macro lenses are generally wonderfully sharp but often react more slowly in autofocus mode than all-purpose lenses. Remember depth of field decreases dramatically when using a lens superclose to the subject!

macro photography. Taking pictures very close in, or of things that are really, really small, like bugs. This often requires specialty lenses (see previous entry), especially for images where the subject appears close to life size in the image.

manual. The booklet that comes in the box with your camera—not "manual exposure" or "manual focus," noble exercises that they are. This is *the* manual. You should read it, and you should take it with you. I am not embarrassed to admit I pack manuals when I travel. They stash conveniently in a bag, take up no room and weigh nothing, but, man, can they save your butt in the field. So, when you get the camera, read the manual. Take it in bite-size pieces. Then, when you confront some perplexing situation in the field, go back and read the section that pertains to it again. And again. This will make your future responses more intuitive and fluid. As with many things in life: Read about it, do it, read some more and keep doing it. You'll get better at it. Guaranteed.

memory card. The storage devices for digital images; the images can be erased, and the cards reused many times. The most common memory cards are Secure Digital (SD) and Compact Flash (CF). I'm not going to write a paper on the performance characteristics of these different cards, but there are some things you should know.

Depending on which camera you decide to purchase, it will use either SD or CF. SD cards can store a lot of photos, but their "speed" is generally slower than CF cards. These cards scare me because they are so small, but they are generally dependable and have adequate storage capacities.

Most professional-model cameras will use CF cards, which nowadays have high storage capacities and fast write speeds. Pro shooters are all about speed; they want the images to move quickly through the camera buffer to the card, and they demand that the card then quickly download imagery to a computer. CF cards are ideal for this, and manufacturers compete to bring faster and faster cards to the market.

For most purposes, here's the best advice I can give: Use a name-brand card. There are lots of knockoff flash memory and memory cards out there. They will corrupt easily, and you will lose images. Dependable cards will cost a bit more, but you don't want to lose your kid's first-place finish at the state track finals to a bad card.

metadata. Information, such as camera settings and exposures, embedded directly into a digital image file. All of the information accompanying captions in this book is metadata.

meter (metering). The meter is the device that measures the amount of light in the frame—or parts of the frame—that you're trying to shoot, and metering is the act of gauging and using this device. It wasn't too long ago that in-camera meters were notoriously undependable. That fact necessitated the use of handheld meters, which were generally quite good. Now, however, the in-camera metering systems of DSLRs are very, very good. Highly sophisticated and sensitive, these meters will give a fine result most of the time.

There are options for meter modes as well. *Multipart or matrix meter mode* will look at all or most of a scene while evaluating the proper exposure response. But you can also shift the meter into *center-weighted metering mode*, which looks at the middle of the picture, or *spot-metering mode*, which looks at just a small spot when taking the reading. An appropriate scenario for using center-weighted metering is a backlit situation, in which the camera has a tendency to be influenced by the bright light behind the subject and therefore renders the subject dark. The center-weighted aspects of this mode will favor that darker subject matter and strive to render the subject properly. Spot-metering mode evaluates just a minuscule area in the whole frame. This is handy during, say, a theater production, when the whole stage is dark save for the lone dancer or actor in a bright spotlight.

mirror lockup. A feature allowing you to lock the little mirror inside your camera up and out of the way after the scene is composed and focused. When you look through your camera, you see the scene via this mirror, which is in front of the sensor. For every exposure you make, that mirror has to swing up and out of the way, which can produce tiny amounts of vibration within the camera. This is not crucial when shooting at fast shutter speeds but is potentially damaging for precise, critical work such as closeup photos and long exposures. Mirror lockup prevents potential loss of sharpness owing to minute amounts of shake, rattle and roll produced by mirror motion.

noise. A "noisy" file is one that is filled with digital grain, or noise (which does not mean loud, raucous color—often a good thing). Noise basically looks like mushy, grainy, weird color blotches in your picture. Poor exposure control can lead to noise in your pictures, as can high ISO and long exposures, such as those

employed during nighttime shooting. Some cameras have in-camera noise-reduction features that are designed to eliminate noise buildup. There are also software programs you can use after the fact, in postproduction.

normal lens. A lens with a focal length around 50mm, the middle ground between wide-angle, shorter lenses and telephoto, longer lenses. Normal lenses produce pictures that look normal, as though the viewer were standing where the camera was held.

overexposure. Too much light hitting the sensor. Overexposure produces a file, or photo, that has very little detail and appears bleached or washed out. Predictably, underexposure produces the opposite effect.

panning. A technique to convey motion. During the exposure, the camera is moved, or "panned," with the subject. Done properly, this results in a sharp subject and a blurry, or "moved," background. Showing motion with a still camera is hard to do, but this approach can get across the idea of a fast-moving subject. A couple of things to be aware of: Your shutter speed has to be set to allow blur. Very fast shutter speeds stop everything. Recommended panning speeds are from 1/60th of a second all the way to 1/8th or 1/4th of a second, depending on the speed of the subject. Another thing: Panning works best with a crossing subject, not one that is approaching the lens or moving away from it. A crossing subject will stay in the same line of distance, relative to the camera position, and thus will require no change of focus.

Also—be aware of your backgrounds. Panning works best if the blurry background is uncluttered and somewhat subdued in tonality.

panoramic camera. A specialized camera that takes in extremely elongated fields of view. Also called a wide-format camera, it generally has an aspect ration of 4:1 and higher, covering a field of view of up to 360 degrees. Sometimes just referred to as a "pano camera."

pixel. Pixels are the tiny dots that—in very large numbers—make up a digital picture. The term pixel stands for "picture element." This isn't a technical explanation, but I tend to think of a digital snap as a giant mosaic: All of these millions of multicolored bits combine to create a densely detailed representation of what you saw.

post-processing. These are all of the things that you do (or could do) to your photographs after you take them but before you print or publish them. The modern world of post-processing and the manipulation of photographs is sometimes referred to as the "digital darkroom," a realm of delight and illusion. All digital pictures generally require some postproduction, which can take the form of basic retouching work, such as sharpening, burning and dodging, increasing or decreasing saturation or contrast adjustment. (Note: Some of those terms are right from the old-style black-and-white darkroom in the basement.) There are vast numbers of post-processing

adjustments now available through extremely powerful software programs such as Photoshop, Aperture and Lightroom, to name but three. With these programs, an experienced retoucher can completely alter the look and feel of a photograph, eliminating and adding elements, changing color tones, extending color schemes and backgrounds and introducing special effects. A picture can be made to have little remaining relation to the real-world scene originally rendered.

prime lens. This is a lens that does not zoom, or, in other words, a single-focal-length lens. Historically these lenses were considered better optically than zooms, which tended to be slower, darker and less sharp than primes. Nowadays, zooms are generally considered to be just as good as primes. Primes are still important, though, as some of these fixed-focal-length lenses will be considerably "faster" than most zooms. Examples would be such lenses as a 24mm f1.4 or a 50mm f1.4 or a 200mm f2. If you want maximum aperture for low-light conditions, or minimal depth of field for selective focus, primes are an excellent option.

raw file. A digital file format that contains untouched, "raw" pixel information straight from the camera's sensors. *See* JPEG.

reflector. Anything you can get your hands on that reflects light. It can be a formal, store-bought piece of gear, like a Tri-Grip reflector, or it can be a piece of cardboard lined with white copier

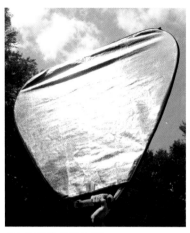

Joe McNally TriGrip Kit

paper. The board can also be wrapped in aluminum foil for a tremendous "bounce" of light. (Obviously, a white board will be subtler.) There are reflectors out there that have shiny gold surfaces. The light reflected by these will be warm in tone and have a slightly yellowish cast.

resolution. This, the number of pixels contained in a digital image, is the salient statistic in today's pixel wars. One camera comes out with a billion pixels, the next feels compelled to counter with two billion, a number professing to yield far superior sharpness and clarity. My opinion? We've all got enough pixels. Forget the numbers. Just go shoot pictures. Make them good. The pixels will love you for it, and they'll do their part.

Rule of Thirds. This is a basic rule of composition, good to have in the back of your head when you are sizing up a scene. Ever play tic-tac-toe? X's and O's? Imagine seeing that grid dropped into your viewfinder. Then you have the Rule of Thirds, horizontally and vertically. It is a dynamic, visually interesting way to frame a scene. Look at each square, and see what's in it. Look at your primary subject, and perhaps place it out of the center, building dynamic relationships with secondary subjects that then come into play elsewhere. Remember, though: This is one of our rules without absolute rules. Don't pass up a good photo just because it doesn't set itself up in the Rule of Thirds grid. And if a subject demands the center by sheer force, yield to it—and you'll be happy with the result.

selective focus. A technique in which the photographer keeps the subject in sharp focus and everything else in the frame fuzzy and out of focus. It's a wonderful way to direct your viewers' attention to right where you want them to look. When using the selective focus technique, and the subject matter is the human face, make sure that the point of critical focus is on the eyes.

self-timer. An option that inserts a delay between the moment you depress the shutter release and the instant the camera takes the picture. If you want to put yourself in the group shot, or record your presence at the Grand Canyon, this is the way to do it and has been for a long time—since well before the digital age. How long to program the delay for? Well, how fast can you run?

sensor. Basically, this is digital "film." It's the device in the camera that records the image you see and converts that into ones and zeroes, or an electrical signal. There are a couple of different types, one being a CCD (charge-coupled device) and another popular one called a CMOS (complementary metal-oxide semiconductor). By comparison, Kodachrome just sort of rolls off the tongue, but the good news is, you don't really have to worry about what's in there, other than to be mindful of . . .

sensor cleaning. This is something that must be done periodically, otherwise your sensor, and hence your image, will look like a car windshield after driving on the highway on a hot Georgia night. Splatter and splotches everywhere. Many camera manuals will tell you to send your camera into the manufacturer's service center for sensor cleaning. Which is fair enough, but also turns a three-minute do-it-yourself exercise into a several-day (or several-week) interval during which you don't have your camera.

Typically, the dust we see on our photos isn't environmental dust, as one would think. More often than not, it's actually metal shavings that come from taking lenses on and off the lens mount. Because a sensor is an electronically charged device, when you take a photo and the mirror exposes it, those metal shavings can very easily get sucked right in. Obviously, the last thing you want is to spend tons of time "de-spotting" your picture. (Cleaning up one picture

is no big deal. But if you are shooting dozens or hundreds of pictures at your niece's wedding, cleaning them up will become a black hole for your time.)

In other words, if you shoot a lot, learning to clean a sensor is essential. At my studio, we use a cleaning kit made by a company called Visible Dust. The kit consists of an LED-lined loupe to see inside your camera, a brush to clean the sensor, as well as swabs and a cleaning solution, should you need to go further. As with all things photographic, there are many different methods and products out there for cleaning sensors, and there are also online tutorials to coach you. Or you could go in for a quick lesson at your local camera shop. The main thing is to overcome your fear of messing with that delicate piece of electronics known as the sensor. Relax. When you clean the surface, you are actually cleaning what's called a low-pass filter that lays over the sensor. You never touch the actual element. I guarantee that, with practice and caution, you'll get the hang of this very necessary task.

shooter. Photog slang for "photographer." As in, "He's a good shooter."

shutter. The tiny device that, when closed, keeps light away from the sensor. Think of it as a curtain on a window: Opening the shutter means you are taking a picture. The shutter is the curtain over the sensor. Open the curtain, light comes in, close the curtain, light goes away, you make a picture. Simplicity itself!

shutter speed. This simply refers to the duration of an exposure. Fast speeds are usually 1/250th of a second up to 1/8,000th of a second, and these fast shutter speeds are generally used in bright conditions. Darker environments demand slower shutter speeds, ranging down from 1/30th of a second or so all the way to 8 or 10 seconds, depending on subject matter. Shutter speed is a critical issue because it will directly impact how sharp your photos are. The slower the shutter, the more chance of camera shake. Shooting sharp at slow shutter speeds requires practice. *Dragging shutter* refers to lengthening your shutter speed as the conditions get darker. As in, "It got so dark out there I had to drag my shutter all the way to 1/4th of a second!"

sidelighting. Lighting whose source is located to the side of the photograph's subject or subjects. Duh!

soft lighting. Diffuse or relatively dim lighting that doesn't create dark or clearly delineated shadows. Think cloudy day. Think soft window light in a pub.

stopping down. This is the process of making the f-stop smaller, which means clicking toward the bigger numbers, which means making the aperture (hole in the lens) tinier. Stopping down the lens allows in progressively less light.

teleconverter. This small, barrel-like tube contains its own lens element that couples the main lens and the camera together and increases the focal length of the lens. Used for telephoto work, it can take a 300mm lens and make it function as a 400, 500, 600 and more, depending on how powerful the teleconverter is. Caution: Purchase a teleconverter made by your own camera system. Third-party teleconverters tend to degrade sharpness and lens performance. Also, be aware that teleconverters cost you in terms of f-stop. Usually, you will lose at least one f-stop or more, again, depending on the conversion factor of the teleconverter.

telephoto lens. This lens with a very long focal length is able to magnify— or zoom in—on distant objects. A telephoto lens lets your eyeball travel across the street or onto the field. This lens has to be held and handled carefully or many out-of-focus pictures will result.

tripod. A three-footed device upon which a camera can be mounted for increased stability. As I've written, I have a love-hate relationship with my tripod. I hate to carry it, feel limited and less than fluid when my camera is locked down on it and, then, when I realize how badly I need it right then and there, I am passionate about it. When I leave it behind out of laziness and then need it, I get mad at it, not me. Tripods are a pain to carry around. They draw attention and often prove unnecessary. But tripods do what they claim: They give you a stable platform to shoot from, define your camera's point of view and are worth their weight in gold in the beautifully murky predawn light when you don't have a prayer of holding your lenses steady.

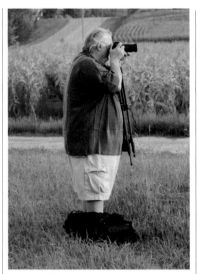

Perhaps this is not the best use of a tripod. Tripods are stablest when they are set up firmly on the ground.

Buy a good tripod—a name brand. The reputable manufacturers often give you a lifetime warranty.

underexposure. An effect achieved when there is not enough light in a photo. The opposite of overexposure. Measured underexposure (like measured overexposure) can be useful, producing a desired, calculated effect. Serious underexposure produces a muddy file, dark and without sharp detail.

view camera. This is a bulky camera with an accordionlike attachment between the lens and the viewfinder, capable of producing truly grandiose imagery. The historically significant view camera has long been associated with Ansel Adams types who own pickup trucks, super-sturdy tripods and constitutions that allow them to get up very early in the morning and set out for places like Yosemite National Park, where, if you get in their way with your quick-as-a-wink digital camera, you will hear about it.

viewfinder. You look through this when you shoot. The more expensive camera models have 100 percent viewfinders, meaning that what you see is what you get. Other models don't show the whole frame, perhaps about 95 per-cent or so of it. This can lead to surprises later in the digital darkroom. So be careful when using your viewfinder.

vignetting. The term refers to a gradual darkening of your image at the corners and edges. There is no need to worry much about this with today's highly engineered lenses, but there are cameras out there, including certain panoramic cameras, that produce significant vignetting that needs to be corrected. One reason I tape my lens shades to the barrel of the lens in the proper position: If you are walking and you bump the shade out of its optimum position, a very visible vignette pattern at the edges of the frame could be the result. You will most likely shoot several frames before you notice the uneven shadows; if you have not experienced this before, you might think your camera is screwing up or is broken.

white balance. A process by which the photographer strives to "correct" lighting conditions so that colors appear lifelike whatever the type of light in which the photograph was made. Light has color, and different lights have different colors. Daylight has different color casts depending on time of day and atmospheric conditions. Artificial light also has particular color casts, such as fluorescent, which gives a distinct green tinge to images. With a digital camera, you can compensate for these different color casts by clicking a dial.

The camera's brain is fine-tuned and adaptive, so there is a white-balance feature called "auto" in most cameras. This means the machine itself will sense the environment it is looking at and try to return to you a pleasingly neutral result. This mode works fairly well in many scenarios, but not all. Experiment with white balance. Dialing in the "wrong" white balance in certain situations may give you interesting results—as has been discussed.

Also, if you are shooting raw files, you can change things up later in the computer. I have heard many times, "Hey, I'm shooting raw, it doesn't matter what white balance I use!" That's fair enough, but as with elements of composition, it usually pays to correct white balance in the field, arriving at the appropriate settings when you are out there with the camera in your hands. First, it will save you time: You won't have to make all those color shifts later in the computer. But more important: Being aware of light—its moods and colors, its qualities and intensities—is part and parcel of becoming a good shooter.

wide-angle lens. A lens with a relatively short focal length but an extended field of view. As we discussed at length in our section on lenses, wide-angles are essential, but dangerous, and can sometimes prove useful in situations that might surprise us, such as portraiture.

zoom lens. A lens with a variable focal length. There are, predictably, wide-angle and telephoto zooms, which cover essential focal lengths at either end of the scale. Both are pretty indispensable. The beauty of modern zooms is that many are so good and so efficient that you, the shooter can go out with just two lenses in your bag and feel covered for just about any situation.

INDEX